This book would not have been possible without the encouragement of Barbara Sweeney.
I thank her for her belief in *One*, her insight and expertise.

> 'We have a stake in one another, and what binds us together is greater than what drives us apart'.
>
> Barack Obama

I love the title of this page. Mainly because content can mean satisfaction, to one's heart's content. It also implies what's contained within. In this case what you may expect from these pages. The conversation that follows is really grassroots stuff. Honouring and understanding oneself, and making the most of life. Embracing the luxury of one; encouragement to enjoy the calm and peace available to you; acknowledging that the only true demands you have come from yourself; it prompts you to make time to be creative; celebrates that you can go where you like, how you like and that it's perfectly okay to do things alone.

It's an affirmation of self. A book about living as one and loving it. My photographs are from everywhere, all over, and mixed up to remind you and me that we are all one. Wherever we're from. Wherever we may be going.

We all share a desire to find contentment. My hope is that you too know we have one thing in common: a need to be able to count on ourselves.

Without wanting to moralise or trivialise it's about life's little lessons — listening to yourself; trying anything on for size; taking risks; valuing the making of a home; asking for what you want; and discouraging others from judging you; life's changes and shifts; enjoying transition and reinventing yourself. It sees that work is an extension of yourself but not a metaphor for who you are or who you should be seen to be. It acknowledges the importance of people believing in you and feeling included.

It's not just for those who live alone. I acknowledge every one has a need for space, to keep a little of themselves for themselves. We all need to have our own sense of self worth. I hope it will encourage you in your acceptance of who you are, who you can be. It's the kind of book where you may find a connection to travel, photography, architecture, people or memories. It would be the ultimate compliment if you left it lying around to tell others 'I am happily a one, my life is what it is, and please don't judge me, thank you very much'. Or better still, share it with a one you love.

The information in this book has been gathered from a lifetime of experience living as one of six (the family I grew up in), five (my married family life), four (life as a single mother), three (as my children left home), two (as a wife), and now as a one.

I have a utopian view of life and believe wholeheartedly in sharing so this book follows that theme. A whole to pick up and put down at will. To look at and read in no particular order. We all have two voices and so does this book. One speaks of my musings, the other voice knows the things I should do, but being human don't always do. If I did my life would be perfect. Choosing pages at whim should give you a feeling of living in the moment, to reflect my belief that there is never a right time or a wrong time. Just now. I didn't want you to lose your place, or train of

thought, in a continuum of pages. It's okay to start from the back. It reflects the way I seem to have lived my life: studying after a career, living alone after marriage.

We ones make up at least one-third of the population and the world feels out of kilter with this reality. Statistically, the numbers of those living alone continues to grow. Despite this you don't have to look far to realise most packaging and advertising, including holidays, don't speak to ones. Ask yourself why are a one-third minority being ignored? I suppose you could say it's just the way it is, the way it has been. I say things need to change for ones to feel valued.

Someone I used to work with told me she felt invisible because she was single. When I mentioned I was writing this book she responded the way many others did: it's needed. My starting point was to give voice to those who are single. I'm aware being a one is equally important when you are in a relationship so it's also the middle and the end game. A desire to be acknowledged and treated as an equal is the same for everyone, no matter what their relationship status is. Along with words and images, I toyed with the title for the book being 'Everyone'. After all, we are all ones, despite our apparent differences, we are individuals, originals, and there is no standard issue for relationships.

I have the feeling I'm not the only one who feels that walking into a party as a single person can lack dignity, that the loss of spontaneity I experienced when moving from managing a family to a one meant understanding a different set of rules. While reorientating myself I found cooking for one an unwanted and major change. I have learnt how to negotiate life differently, to follow my own instincts. The world is full of stories much like mine — often hushed because there's a sense of shame about being a one. A veil. This seems unnecessary and a silent protest won't change anything.

HFR962

A preoccupation about everyone having a relationship prevails. Signs and expectations we share our lives are everywhere. Throwaway lines in the media and endless 'I got my man' films. At times it can feel all the evidence around you provides proof that all the world's a couple, except you. So it's important to realise things are not always as they seem. Those twosomes you assume are couples may just be family enjoying each other's company. Or friends. I love the thought of those couples successfully married for thirty or forty years who credit a large part of their success to maintaining their individuality. Their oneness if you like. Their sense of their own self worth is valuable to them.

Living alone is a clear choice for some. A conscious decision to be a one; they like it and intend to keep it that way. They know half of all first marriages end in divorce. Other ones avoid commitment because of education or a career. For some it's just what life delivered. Simple as that. It's not a choice; it's partly circumstantial, may be statistical, nature's sex balance.

Not so long ago there were three main living arrangements: living with our parents; living with a partner and perhaps some of this time with children; and living alone in old age. This has reversed as we generally live alone or in a group household before partnering. Many people also live either alone or with one parent after a divorce, separation, or death. In future more people are likely to live alone as the typical household of a married couple with children is a thing of the past. Marriage rates have declined, divorce rates increased. Other changes in demographic and social trends include declining fertility, delayed starts to family life, and increased life expectancy. We are constantly evolving because of direct or indirect reactions to circumstances: changes around birth, a loss, moving, work and life experiences. And expectations.

It's not uncommon to be nervous when going it alone. But it's not worth having a meltdown over. Being solo can be thrilling and daunting in equal measure. When I moved house and began living alone my brother, who had lived as one for a while, counselled me. He offered a warning not to rush into another relationship, that I may just learn to love reading the paper undisturbed, while eating breakfast in my pyjamas. Not having to answer to somebody else was a luxury I had not yet known. Sage advice.

I've learnt being a one offers freedom along the road toward contentment. When that search is rewarded everything else seems to fall into place and the most enviable and important thing of all happens, you feel at one with yourself. You can go places when and how you choose, eat or buy whatever you want to without having to consider anyone else. Living alone also means you're the one who always gets to put the rubbish out. To pay the bills. To change the lightbulbs. And restock.

Standing at an airport counter as a one, just minutes after the manifest has closed, arguing your case to be allowed to board your plane, is a totally different experience to standing there with the power of two. Is it simply because the authority feels outnumbered? Or is it that you feel you have support and so can argue more persuasively?

Depending on who lives next door we may forget the bible's warning not to covet thy neighbour's wife. To want another's life, one that looks all daffodils and roses from the outside, is unrealistic. Covetousness is a contemporary plague and the growth in materialism has bought neither reassurance nor contentment, but unrealistic aspirations and competitiveness that do little to maximise the sum of human happiness.

There's no assurance of what the future holds for any of us. Just like cooking, you have to trust your own instincts. It takes confidence, practice and patience and this needs building as a one. It can't be taught and needs to grow from experience as you work out what's important for you. Others want you to be happy, for you to have someone in your life in an 'then you'll be one of us' kind of way. But everybody knows the best things in life are the simple things. Living alone can make things as simple or as complicated as you like.

We are all members of one tribe or another and, so it seems, must be defined. This definition is part of who we feel we are. The dictionary meaning of single is 'one only; separate; alone'. When used for describing yourself I hope you'll agree using 'only' is objectionable. A similar feeling applies when someone says being single is a waste. It is as if being on your own is not living life to the full.

I've a proposition for you. Let's begin our journey through this book together by changing the terms 'single' or 'they live alone' to I'm, they're, he, or she's

'a one'.

Wouldn't it be fun to tick ☐ One
rather than Single, Divorced or Widow on forms to state you enjoy life and are not defined by your past? Being labelled as part of a singles tribe feels wrong. As a mother I feel very connected to my children. I have also enjoyed a married life. I know the feeling of being introduced as someone's other half, and so the implication that something or someone is missing, or that I am incomplete, doesn't fit.

Without wanting to sound too Californian about it, the way we treat ourselves is the most important thing there is. A label that fits, empowers and delivers an acceptance of me or you, as one, seems a wonderful possibility.

We 'ones' are busy making the most of things, are accepting of our current romantic status, and are happy with who we are. We object to well-meaning questions like 'Have you met anyone yet?' (yet, as if it is only a matter of time and an assured thing you will or want to) or 'Do you have anyone in your life?' (Yes, thank you. I have a full and joyful life and am loved). For some ones it's not that we wouldn't appreciate a loving and intimate presence in our lives, it's just that there is not that chance right now, we know that longing for it is a waste of valuable one time. For others it is their choice, a preference.

But, best of all, being a one offers the chance to celebrate your uniqueness, to get to know yourself without having to please anyone else. It's not a selfish life. Coming to terms with, and accepting, who you are and what you are capable of, without relying on anyone else for fulfilment is empowering. It enables you to be whole. It's up to you to join in and make this happen. Please do.

Describe your **marital status** by ticking the appropriate box

- ☐ single
- ☐ spinster
- ☐ bachelor
- ☐ unmarried aunt
- ☐ defacto
- ☐ widow
- ☐ divorcee
- ☐ desperate
- ☐ not desperate
- ☐ farmer who wants a wife

- ☐ one

Much more than one

ME
YOU
SELF
SOLO
FIRST
ALONE
OLDEST
SINGLE
FREEDOM
SINGULAR
SOLITARY
IDENTITY
ONLY ONE
JUST ONE
INDIVIDUAL
NUMBER ONE
NATIONALITY
ON YOUR OWN
JUST FOR ONE?
SINGLE HANDED
LOSS OF PLURAL
GOING IT ALONE
ONE TRACK MIND
THE POWER OF ONE
TWENTY-ONE = ADULT
'IT'S NOT ALL ABOUT YOU'

Single

In the record industry a single was cause for celebration.
One song, usually from a current album,
released to promote the album.
This one track, part of a collective, told the story.
If it did well, so usually did the whole.
Now you're able to make your own mix of singles.

One moment

Said with a smile.
'I loved the drive.
Four hours to myself.
Space opened up,
the countryside is beautiful.
I was in my own world.
Time without anyone.'

Another moment

'I'm dreading the drive home.
I'm tired,
have a bit of a headache.
Wish I could share the driving.'
Smiles fade.

Beginnings

Family is the base from which we learn to walk
into our own life.
A life where we are free to choose.
But no matter what family remain,
psychologists believe birth order is a big part of who we are.
They believe it has a profound and lasting effect
on our development.
Neil Armstrong, the first man to walk on the moon,
is a first born. So too were 21 of the first 23 astronauts to go into space.
If that doesn't tell you something, then knowing the
other two were only children may.
You don't have to be the oldest child in your family
to take the lead in your life.

Parenting is a vital role.
At the start it's easy to be overwhelmed with the responsibility,
no matter how much you wanted it.
Your ability unfolds as trust and confidence build.

As parents we are accountable for our children's actions.
We need to ensure they have the tools to cope and grow on their own.
We need to understand what they are going through,
to be empathetic, provide support and to teach them ethics.
It's a challenge to learn more about them and to
let them know more about you.
Sometimes it feels as if you are giving more than you get.
Which is not such a bad thing.

Balancing roles, home and work, ensuring there is
enough love to go around, that you don't feel guilty because you
should be somewhere else, and finding a routine that works for you
are things many of us grapple with.

During a working day we are in control of a lot of things.
There are people to turn to for advice; mentors to lean on and role models to admire.
We are rewarded for our work.
The rewards at home are not always as obvious.
They are long term.

Family you choose

Sometimes friends become family.
You rely on them in the same way.
Value their advice.
They would do anything for you.
And do.
And you for them.
They pick you up when you are down.
Stop you driving when you shouldn't.
Share all they have.
Including Christmas.
It makes you feel good just to see them.
The world's a better place due to them.

A good meal is the most trusted currency in the world.
Preparing food is an ancient craft that's a central part
of any culture.
Each time I'm lucky enough to eat at a Thai, Vietnamese,
Chinese, Italian, French, Greek or Persian restaurant
I can't help but think how lucky we are to be able to access
different cultures through food.
It's a wonderful exchange, easier to comprehend than language,
and a way of travelling vicariously.
I also think of the heritage of the people who made my meal.
Often these enterprising people who run the
restaurant or café include all of the family
in their business and have left their homeland to start again.
Lucky for us food culture is transportable.
We are richer for it.

I'm fortunate to live in a multicultural city, one with great diversity; especially in its food offerings. You can eat Italian one day, Greek the next and Chinese the following should you choose. So unlike others who experience hunger and have few or no options I can travel vicariously when I want to. I appreciate that having the option to travel has helped make me who I am. Being welcomed in another culture is for me one of the greatest privileges that exists.

The anticipation of a trip is exciting. I love the research, the planning and reading about foreign places before I go. When I get back I adore walking into my home because for one moment it feels like somewhere new and I see it as others must. Downloading and scrolling through my photos I notice things all over again. But most of all it is people who have made my travel experiences memorable. The appreciation of the individual; that we are all first of all a person before a nationality. It's our families and our culture that bind us together and shape us.

I saved, and saved, for my first trip at twenty-one, and with a little help from an inheritance, travelled with two friends around Europe and Scandinavia for $5 a day. I took six months off work, and, with a map that became dog-eared and one guidebook, we went where we wanted and stayed as long as we liked. By putting myself into the world and outside my comfort zone I found I was connected to the human race in more ways than I had realised. The connectedness was in the daily rhythm of things. By joining in with other cultures' ways of life and engaging in our differences and similarities prejudices disappear and we can begin to understand each other. If we look at ourselves and others non-judgmentally we can live loving, compassionate lives.

This first trip to Europe included seeing my brother compete in the Olympics. Racism, intolerance and war are harder to comprehend once you have watched all but a few countries march together in a confined space, swap smiles, addresses and team sweaters. Surely travelling makes others wish for greater harmony too?

For years I put off going to India because I thought the poverty I'd encounter would disturb me in a way that would make me feel helpless. As my children put it, I'd be sure to come back with a few extra children. Instead I found being among people who make much of little inspiring. India's beauty is immense in many different ways, the colour joyful. Their sense of community, the spiritual choices they treasure and celebrate, their respect for the elderly, the way they wrap babies in silk like gifts, and their close and intimate housing that demands they show consideration for each other, all add up to a treasure trove for the senses. They are inclusive and their smiles ready. That's not to say it's easy to turn a blind eye to those who are hungry and I know India is not enjoyable for everyone, but I love it because it taught me not to judge.

India has not been my only teacher. Travel experiences are a chance for reflection and have provided valuable lessons, not just in compassion. Travelling has taught me to observe. I have a heightened attention to all around me. Finding myself in unexpected places and circumstances makes me in awe of the freedom I have. It is a privilege to have stood in postcard-perfect places. I have pondered history, felt the wisdom of old and been reminded of all that is and isn't possible while driving alongside the Golan Heights. Sauntering through Bhutanese Dzongs free of outside influences and into a street where an entire mountain village was manicuring the street with twig brooms in a manner that felt like a Buddhist meditation was a reminder of the simple, pure things in life, and the importance of community. In Bhutan, by royal decree, all men are forbidden to wear trousers in public and so wear a *gho*, an often checked or plaid knee-length dress, with a sash at the waist, and long stockings. If you are caught wearing anything else, you pay a fine, equal to about three-days pay. This is in order to preserve their unique national culture and assimilate ethnic minorities. The women have a similar distinctive way of dressing, a full-length dress called the *kira*. Their palette and uniformity of dress made me feel I was a part of a Himalayan Bruegel painting.

Floating down the muddy Mekong at sunset, in a turquoise and red wooden boat, so bright it made you feel good just to look at it, watching fisherman expertly cast their nets while standing knee or waist deep in water, feels a long way away from a restaurant's daily fish deliveries. Wandering past the long rows of perfectly laid brickwork apartments in the narrow canal streets of Amsterdam, I've wondered why more of the world can't rely on bicycles and then remembered just how flat this city is. Traversing a Mayan site in Mexico with an expert close at

hand to willingly share all he knows about Mexican and Cuban history is one of the best possible lecture theatres. Coming across elderly people dancing in the street outside office buildings during an early morning walk, something I discovered they do as a daily ritual in Shanghai, was a display of the energy and joy of life that some have. African plains are observatories for life at its most real.

My curiosity and appreciation of beauty have been heightened by taking part in daily life in a market square doused with soft French or Italian light. I've reflected on how a simple material, tissue paper, can be used so differently in the hands of different cultures when watching primary-coloured flags, cut by hand, flutter freely across a Mexican street, and again when observing saffron-robed monks light the candles in rainbow-coloured lanterns as they hung from hundred- year-old trees in Luang Parbang. I marvelled at their silence and discipline again the next morning as about three hundred or so monks walked silently in single file around the village to collect alms from kneeling villagers. I promised myself I too could become that peaceful inside.

Travel memories can be uplifting many years on. Remembering the soft melodic voice of my Indian guide explain Hindu beliefs makes for feeling connected to others. Catching an unmistakeably Cuban sound waft though the balmy air means I can access that energised spirit again and be uplifted every time I listen to that type of music. Walking along a narrow cobbly street in Morocco with its high walls and heartbreakingly beautiful, shabby buildings on each side and through the world's oldest cities, Damascus and Aleppo, with their their Ottoman houses overhanging the tiny lanes, I felt they had something in common. The smell of

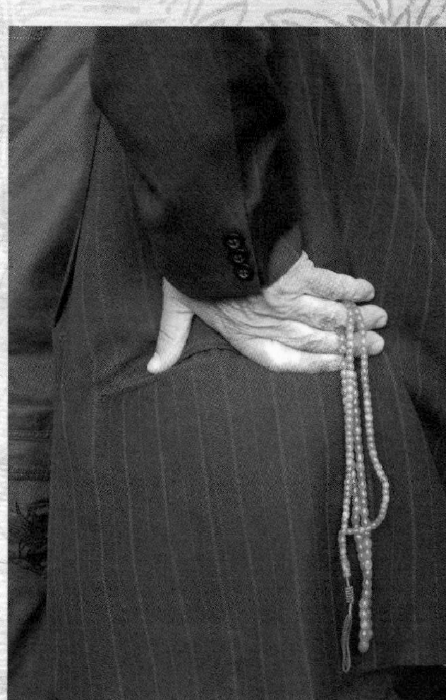

cooking with tomatoes, cumin and cinnamon wafting through a window. I've found police uniforms have a habit of looking like dress-ups, red buses like toys and eucalyptus always feel like home.

Travel heightens our points of difference. It's a wonder Jews, Muslims, Hindus, and Buddhists don't cross out Christian on entry and exit forms that should ask for your first name. When telling friends I was going to Syria, Jordan and Iran the common reaction was 'Why? Won't it be dangerous because of the political instability?' I'd done my research and felt secure I was in safe hands as I was travelling with a friend who has been an archaeologist on digs in the area for about thirty years. He loves it. So my reply: 'Why not?' I had a desire to understand first hand what it feels like to be in a beautiful country, with a complex history and gentle people, judged as unsafe territory by so many. Media reports, often with a political bent, make us hesitate and warn us not to go. Sometimes the risk is not what it seems on the surface and once weighed up can deliver something more memorable than going to a safe territory. I have never been made to feel more welcome. We were endlessly told 'Thank you for coming.' It's a phrase as common as hello. Their instinct is to share. Uttering 'Marhaba' or 'Salam' to anyone will guarantee a quick and warm welcome in response and possibly the offer of tea. Endless freshly brewed small glasses of tea make for wonderful exchanges. Language is no barrier to a carpet seller or perfume vendor in the bazaar.

Visiting Iran, Syria and Jordan also reinforced that things are not always as they seem from a distance. There were no disappointments, just wonderful daily surprises. Middle Eastern history records things way beyond my logical grasp.

It's easy to forget the very first Islamic mosque was designed as a playground. The Umayyad Mosque in Damascus can trace its history back to the third millennium BCE and still operates as one. Children slide smoothly across its cool marble courtyard, pulled in their socks by mothers shrouded in black. Others kick balls while women read together and enjoy a picnic. It's a social place that anchors the evocative backstreets with its magnificent presence, just like a cathedral in Europe. Ruins like Palmyra, spread across a hundred acres, date back to the nineteenth century BCE and are virtually unguarded. Thankfully this reinforced my belief that if you are trustworthy it is easy to trust others.

So did the bus trip we took in Shiraz, Iran, by chance. When our tour bus broke down in the middle of a four lane highway our local guide hailed a passing bus. We quickly boarded through the front and rear doors, the driver would accept no money and happily diverted from his route for about a kilometre or so to our hotel's front door. His segregated passengers, male in the front and female in the rear, welcomed us warmly, did not mind that we had mixed up the sexes, and happily waved goodbye as we departed, elated at the whole experience. Yes there are women cloaked in black, who expose themselves only by their taste in shoes and make-up (though the plentiful lingerie shops tell of another life), but there are almost as many women in skin-tight jeans and body-hugging coats on mobile phones. Men wear suits or large white cotton shirts that keep things looking fresh and no alcohol means the streets are quiet and feel pleasant, even late at night.

Chance meetings are part of the joy of travel. Wandering around Gerasa, in Jerash, Jordan, a city as old as the Bronze Age and often called the Pompeii of the

Middle East, the sun on my back and wildflowers cascading down the hillside, a waft of music and laughter filled the air. Irresistible. I followed the strains of the bagpipes to discover a group of about sixty people, a mini United Nations of the Middle East, dancing in an ancient amphitheatre. All looked university age, and there were too many different styles of traditional dress to be from one country. The rest of the afternoon was spent walking and talking with two from this group, a couple I first thought, in their twenties. Slowly revealed was the group's reason for gathering. Called together, chosen by their country's leaders, they were in Jerash for a youth conference to find ways the Middle East could find peace. The girl, in her twenties, and her chaperone, a male nurse, were both from Saudi Arabia. He, dressed from head to toe in immaculate white, spoke little English, and was clearly not going to leave her side. Her English was perfect, as was the hope in her story. She was a doctor, and proud to disclose she was the first woman to represent her country in this type of delegation, a pilot so she 'could easily get places' and when I said her mother must be proud, her reply was 'It's my father who has encouraged me. I am proud of him.'

The luckiest I have ever felt while travelling was walking around Machu Picchu, a pre-Colombian Inca site that was constructed in AD 1340, it's 2,430 metres above sea level. Protected by UNESCO, the main way to get there is along a winding train track. Some keen ones walk. It's considered a sacred place and it was easy to see why, standing there in the tranquility of those Peruvian mountains. Usually crowded, we were the only three. The train had come off its tracks and nobody else could reach the peak, at least not for a day or two.

There's one common thread I seek out everywhere, markets. They are the first place I head to and they tell much about life in that town or city. The spices, produce and vendors all have local colour that is irresistible. I wonder why we, in Australia, don't have more places where the food is made available in the quantity you want, and not packaged in plastic and polystrene. Rugs draped over walls have led me down alleys, through souqs in Morocco and Istanbul, while the chaos of tiny streets filled with the fragrance of orange blossom in Seville invited me to wonder slowly. The simplicity and functionality in Scandinavian design, their long twilight, and red barns set in bright yellow fields of rape is something I hope to get back to. But first West Africa, Tunisia and Ireland feel as if they have things to teach me that cannot be gained in any lecture theatre, along with the joy of what my lens may find. Oh, to hear the sound of my shutter click on a lush green Irish field with a small white house off to the right or left, or focus on a red and white striped sail on a faluka on a quiet part of the Nile.

My parents travelled. I remember being about nine when my mother bought a new suit and hat to travel in. They were off around the world, as it was then known. There's a black and white photo of them standing beside the departure board, one of those black felt ones with movable white plastic letters that fit in slots. The board has one Qantas flight to London and another to Hong Kong, that's all. It took them days to get to Europe. My dynamic sister, ten years older, was awarded a Fulbright Scholarship and studied in Cambridge, Massachusetts. We used to relish getting the letters that would arrive in blue air-mail envelopes, written in fountain pen on thin crinkly air mail paper, talking of her adventures. She felt far away and I felt envious. My great aunt, Amy, was a great traveller. She was intrepid and had exotic treasures from her travels scattered around her house. Carvings, a doll dressed in green felt with clogs and turned up hat and primitive wooden bowls. Some thirty years ago, using my inheritance from her, I followed in her footsteps to Bali and found a country whose beauty still haunts me, and people who were supremely gracious and open. She used to paint her memories of places and I imagine she has had a subconscious influence on my desire to see the world and learn to understand it.

Deserts make you feel small, rolling hills of olive trees restore you, and landscapes feel familiar because you recognise that you've seen them before through the eyes of an artist. But airports are another land altogether. Parallel runways lead to all parts of the world while all types of people lounge around, mostly looking dissatisfied. People alone, looking bored as if it's all about business. Frazzled families looking like another minute is way too long together. Sleepers tucked in for the duration. Arriving at an airport is an instant introduction to a country. Men in long white Nubian shirts glide over marble in airports built

to impress, or tall blue-black men lean in a meaningful way in sheds they call airports in Africa. Everyone seems busy respecting each other's space or privacy. I often wonder about the stories we could share if we all started talking. That's what happens when travelling alone or as one in a group. Chance meetings of minds and interests take place. Travelling alone can be an advantage as our responses to the world are critically moulded by whom we are with. Our curiosity and reactions are affected by the expectations of others so it allows for unique experiences and time to do what you please. It brings you closer to who you really are. You can move at an individual pace; make friends with whom you like. Distance between you and those you love teaches self-reliance.

When you travel you always carry yourself with you. There is no such place as far away. Simply places that hold no memories, where nobody knows your name. We are living longer, and have further to travel. In 1900 the average life expectancy was forty-six for women and forty-five for men. The average now is eighty-three years. No wonder the world has a growing number of grey nomads wanting adventure.

Some people consider travel a luxury. I say I would not be the same person without it. I promised myself at twenty-one that I would somehow make a trip once a year. I have kept that promise. I know some people use it as an escape from the real world but for me it has been my greatest teacher. It has taught me about the world and how to to feel safe within my own skin.

1

Giorgio Morandi has heightened my appreciation for the familiar. I first saw his paintings in the Tate Modern, London, and wondered at his ability to arrange and capture pure form. Morandi, a favourite one, was an Italian who believed in the discipline of art. He worked alone in one small room, chosen for its light, while surrounded by the typical Italian mix of family life and ones in the university city of Bologna, Italy. Morandi looked at humble, everyday things with new thinking. He painted the same simple motifs, his 'usual things', repeatedly giving them presence and treating them reverently. He discovered immense complexity within his self-imposed limitations and practiced his art to teach us to see. Until his death in 1964, at the age of seventy-three, he shared the family home with his three unmarried sisters, turning one room into his own complete world. He used the purity of his solitude to perfect his small paintings of bottles, bowls and boxes. Morandi had three subjects; flowers, the objects kept on his shelves, and the landscape seen through his window or the nearby countryside where he explored a limited territory. His subtle motifs changed little and as you get to know his interior landscapes you get to know his subjects. His works are restrained, feel almost private, appear intuitive and deceptively simple due to his use of spatial relationships and the forthright way he executes his colour, tone and balance. They are about real life and are modest. They're not nostalgic. There's a stillness to them and, like all good things, they have grace.

Nothing is more abstract than reality

It's better to lead
a bazaar life
than a bland one

The way you see yourself
is not the same way others see you.

Value being on your own

Value yourself.

Take whatever path will lead you to find contentment.

Enjoy the quieter times.

Get to know who you truly are so that you can share the best of yourself with others.

There is wonderment in finding out who you are, seeing yourself clearly.

Explore yourself.

Not everybody has the same appetite for change.

Often the person who has made the change will not be aware of your feelings as they are caught up in the management of a new life. Don't judge them for it. They are simply using their energy to adapt.

Try to see it from their perspective. Find a different way to keep in touch. Good friends are worth the effort. Life without them would be empty.

Be proactive in finding ways to maintain the connection. Share how you would like to stay in touch and ask them what they prefer. They too will care. Most of all, let them know you are there for them to support them through their new challenges. That way the demands of a friendship won't be a burden but will provide release and be a sounding board. You too can learn from another's new relationship.

It seems all the world imagines people come in pairs.
Or more.
A crowd?

'Only one?'

'Just one?' heard so often.
As if one is incomplete.

One eye sees
The other feels

Paul Klee

It's all about the way we say, or is it see, things

Thinking is really talking to your self
and so the language we use is important.
It involves both a speaker (I)
and a listener (me).
Descartes, the rationalist and
father of modern philosophy
famously said *cogito ergo sum*,
which means I think therefore I exist.
He believed thinking starts with the eye and
came up with his immortal line when alone in bed.
He must have liked his own company.
Whichever way you see things
it's important when you are talking to
yourself that you are true, honest and kind.
Who better to fill your needs?

There was much to celebrate — time spent in the company of friends, a present of tickets to listen to Leonard Cohen live that may well be the best concert experience in my lifetime, and Chinese New Year.

There was the luxury of not having to negotiate with anyone else about how to get there, or where to park, so I decided to take the car. The car park was unusually user friendly, no queue or jostling for a space. Being early, feeling content and lucky, I entered the restaurant to be shown to a table reserved for three. I was first and found myself in Siberia, an affectionate nickname I give to the worst tables. I was seated by the entrance so I was the first thing everyone saw as they arrived. Everyone else in the restaurant was Chinese and so I had a momentary feeling of having been transported to Shanghai. I sat quietly and alone, wondering if they chose to give me the worst table in the restaurant because they thought I was meeting other women and our ordering would be modest before a concert.

For comfort and company I asked for a menu and was amused to see a list of special dishes with auspicious names like 'Golden Opportunity' and 'Happy Future' in honour of the Chinese New Year. We were entering the Year of the Ox, which the waiter told me is 'good for financial'. I filled in time by musing that the auspicious names on the menu augured well for a quick recovery from the Global Financial Crisis of 2009.

After a little while a text arrived from my friends to say they would be another ten or so minutes so please order the wine. This I did along with making mental food choices. I wanted the 'Happy Future'. Being unusually early and my friends unusually late I had time to sit alone feeling like an installation everyone had come to see in an art gallery. It's a familiar feeling, of being obvious when you don't want to be. I used to put it down to my shyness, then I discovered other ones felt the same.

The moment my friends arrived the pace of service and my mood immediately picked up. My red dress and bling were noticed for what they were — a celebration.

Normally I use my arrival tactic. I've learnt to arrive just a little after the due time so that when I walk into a room other people have already arrived. I'm hopeful nobody will notice I'm on my own; similarly when others arrive after me they'll not notice either. It's to avoid that feeling that's akin to the uneasiness of the first day at school or at a new job. That feeling of being obvious for being on your own can happen any and everywhere. Sitting at a table of couples all trying hard not to appear to notice you are, as they put it, 'the odd one out', you ask yourself why does it matter to them? You are hopeful of a good night's conversation just as they are. Those in a relationship have that feeling when hesitantly going to something on their own.

Those who live a true village life are unlikely to be able to identify with this feeling. They cook communally, live a mixed up life of old and young together and are rarely on their own. This feeling of disquiet, as if you are being singled out in a crowd when not wanting to be, can be a mixture of dread and anticipation. That feeling passes, but do we ones need to feel like this?

If the attitude of restaurants and supermarkets changed others would follow. Shopping for food can be frustrating and isolating. Supermarkets rarely sell things packaged for one. Loaves of bread, packets of perishables, pasta and biscuits are sized to last a one for weeks, a family for one meal. The choice of single items is only one reason I adore farmers markets. Specialist providores who understand the value of a smile, recognise a 'regular' and offer freshly produced food fits well within the one philosophy. Shopping this way, basket in hand, has the sense of everyone being an individual about it.

Watch people waiting for someone on the street, outside a restaurant, on a bus or train and you'll see they often fill an uncomfortable gap by texting or talking on their mobile phone. At airports it's laptops. It used to be lighting up a cigarette. Feeling exposed is something most of us have in common. If we acknowledged each other and showed an understanding of this feeling by acting openly in these situations we may begin an empathetic movement, one that encourages acceptance of each other. Smiling at someone for the sake of making their day a little better is reason enough alone. It seems when your face becomes one that shows experience it's easier to get your smiles accepted. But if people of all ages acknowledged each other in a crowd sometimes it would not look so much like the beginning of a pick up line.

There are unspoken comfort zones. Movie houses seem an equaliser. The lights dim and everyone's cocooned in the same cave, having the same conversation. It's a place you'll see people happy on their own. Parks and beaches too.

While I was a restaurateur I felt it was flattering to have someone come and eat on their own. It was clear they wanted what we offered, what we took pride in making, the food and atmosphere, and weren't just in the restaurant for the company of those they were with. A darkly-lit corner table, or one near the toilet doesn't seem remotely suitable for someone with these sentiments. My wish is others will see an advantage in one and take that attitude to the streets, instead of 'that feeling'.

Go on. Go out.

I wish I was one.

Capacity to love

once one is one, no more, no less.

Tom, a great dog who just happens to be my grand-dog, is the prime example of appreciating what he's got. He makes the most of everything. You think he'll be wiry but he's not, he's soft to touch, mid-sized, and of indeterminate breeding. But he's no mutt.

Marked to be 'destroyed' he was saved just in the nick of time. Aged two, he clearly had a history. One he can't share but he doesn't make that our problem.

He settled in quickly and appreciates everything he's got and lets you know it.

He understands friendship, knows the pleasure of spending time together and lives in the moment. He's an appreciator of life's simple joys — the comfiest chair, a tummy rub and finding stray tennis balls during a walk. He trades old ones for newer, fresher ones. He's not so happy to watch you leave, and we are rewarded tenfold when he comes along. His loyalty is unflinching and steadfast.

Just like the rest of us, Tom is a complete, unique individual with the capacity to love and enjoy company. He gives unconditional love, in return for giving us the chance to be kind.

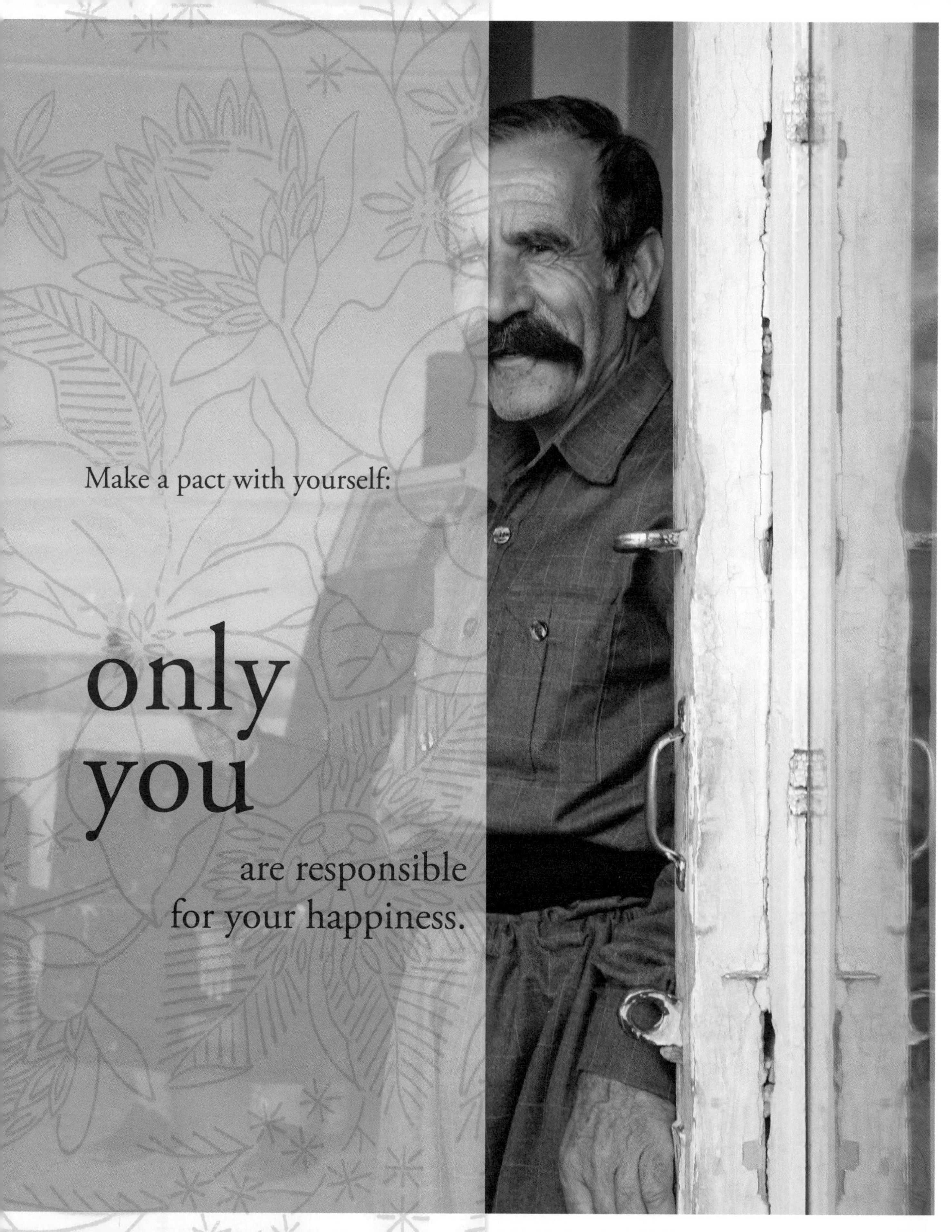

Make a pact with yourself:

only you

are responsible for your happiness.

Leonard Cohen, a Canadian poet, singer, songwriter, musician, and novelist, who can also draw, has been a favourite one since his first record was released in 1967, eleven years after his first book of poetry was published. He is touring worldwide giving concerts in his seventies, wooing people with his poems and songs about sex, spirituality, religion, and power. Leonard speaks of life with an appreciation of how elusive answers can be. There are more than two thousand renditions of his songs, which have a strong emotional force and a beguiling intimacy. Leonard sings them with a unique pace.

Born into a Jewish middle-class family he's studied philosophies and religions 'but cheerfulness kept breaking through'. He has been ordained a Japanese zen Buddhist monk and spent a reclusive two years in a cabin in high desert country, once a boy scout camp. Jikan, his dharma name, means Silent One, he values his privacy as much as his spirituality, has spent years on his own and had some lovers.

'It's just self-respect that you're looking for in your work. You just keep uncovering your own heart until you can find something in which you can locate your self respect … it has to satisfy the heart, the mind and the gut.'

'I have tried in my way to be free.'

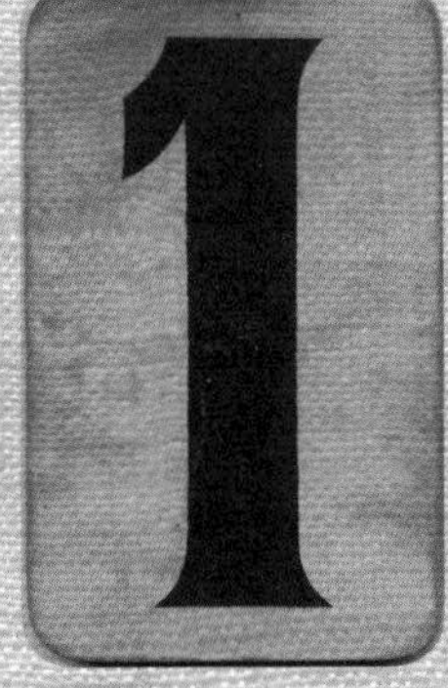

When you live alone

you don't always get a little daily

squeeze, a spontaneous sign of affection

and reinforcement.

This doesn't mean you don't want one.

Remind yourself What revives you? Who inspires you?

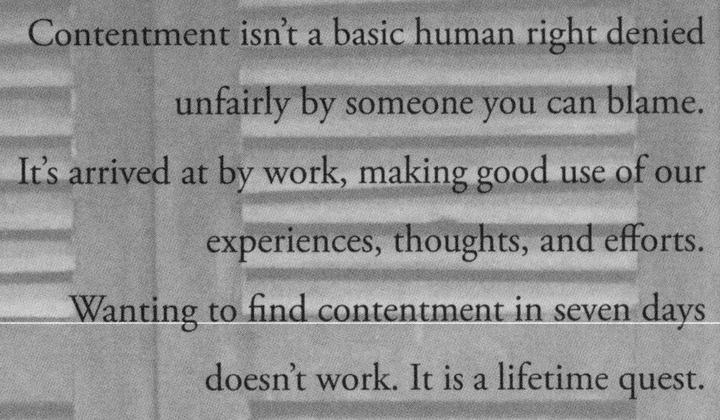

Contentment isn't a basic human right denied unfairly by someone you can blame. It's arrived at by work, making good use of our experiences, thoughts, and efforts. Wanting to find contentment in seven days doesn't work. It is a lifetime quest.

Experience is a springboard that opens doors

We Are Our Own Engineer

We learn how to be when we're growing up.
It comes easily to us when we're little.
We learn a set of rules we use every day.
They become habit.
Until we experience something to change them.
Some rules are intended only as guidelines,
leaving us room to grow.
We can learn something new anytime we believe we can.
We learn there is nobody else exactly like us.
Some people may have some parts that are like us,
but they don't add up the same.
We learn self esteem is essential.
It's the centre of our being.
It makes it possible to act in our best interests.
It also allows us to reinvent ourselves.
To discard the bits we have improved on.
We don't always learn to own our actions.
Our dreams, fantasies, hopes and fears.
As we own all of ourselves it's important
we learn all about ourselves.
To be friendly and loving to ourselves.
To like ourselves so we can love others.
To value the familiar.

I feel like a complete egg

Singular, beautiful and complete.
It's many colours and needs gentle handling.
Being told you're a good egg is a hearty compliment.
Once broken it's hard to repair,
Humpty taught us that.
I guess we all feel like a bit of an egg sometimes.

Raw or tartare ❁ Starting something new.
Scrambled ❁ Confused by someone's behaviour.
Poached ❁ Out of your depth.
Boiled ❁ Settled in for the night.
Fried ❁ Feeling surrounded and edgy.
Omelette ❁ Enjoying friends.
Base for mayonnaise ❁ Being a mother.
Stabiliser ❁ A boss.
Binding ❁ With friends.
Clarifying ❁ Studying or doing research.
Cracked ❁ The end of a relationship.
Eggflip ❁ Nothing is going right.
Rancid ❁ Done over by another's wrong deeds.
Whole ❁ The goodness inside all of us.

Perhaps that's why when tired and alone,
in need of comfort food or simply
wanting an uncomplicated something,
it's a simple egg we reach for.
Boiled mostly.
With soldiers for protection.

I...

- ☐ Enjoy my own company
- ☐ Can survive on my own
- ☐ Relish being an individual
- ☐ Feel at one with myself
- ☐ Am my own best friend
- ☐ Accept who I am and who I can be
- ☐ Believe loving myself is important
- ☐ Feel free to choose what I want my life to be
- ☐ Act unselfishly, show consideration
- ☐ Realise restrictions are often self imposed
- ☐ Live in the present
- ☐ Am prepared to try new things
- ☐ Am not afraid to take risks
- ☐ Don't mind asking for support when needed
- ☐ Realise I'm never alone, I have myself to count on

Ones...

- ☐ Know a relationship is not the only path to happiness
- ☐ Are aware everyone needs space from time to time
- ☐ Are unique, know it and celebrate it
- ☐ Feel comfortable in their own skin
- ☐ Are happy with their own company
- ☐ Use their potential
- ☐ Like who they are
- ☐ Enjoy their freedom
- ☐ Think of other's needs, are empathetic
- ☐ Have healthy self talk
- ☐ Love every moment
- ☐ Are prepared to try new things
- ☐ Take risks
- ☐ Seek help when needed
- ☐ Know the value of solitude

It is possible to

love living on your own.

Some people find themselves alone and don't want to be.

But there can be an upside.
Fewer demands on your time, no annoying mess,
noisy distractions, nights of irritating snoring.
It can mean choosing to get out of bed when you want,
the satisfaction of paying your own bills
and putting out the garbage.
There can be times when you stay in your pyjamas all day.
Luxuries that those who live with others can long for.

It is possible to

love living on your own.

Many people wouldn't have it any other way.

It can mean listening to whatever music you want
without anyone bugging you to turn it down,
eating what you want whenever you like,
staying up all night reading, writing or watching movies,
or spontaneously phoning a friend and talking for hours,
whatever time of day.
And then there are the times when it can be as quiet as a library.
A solitude those who live with others long for.

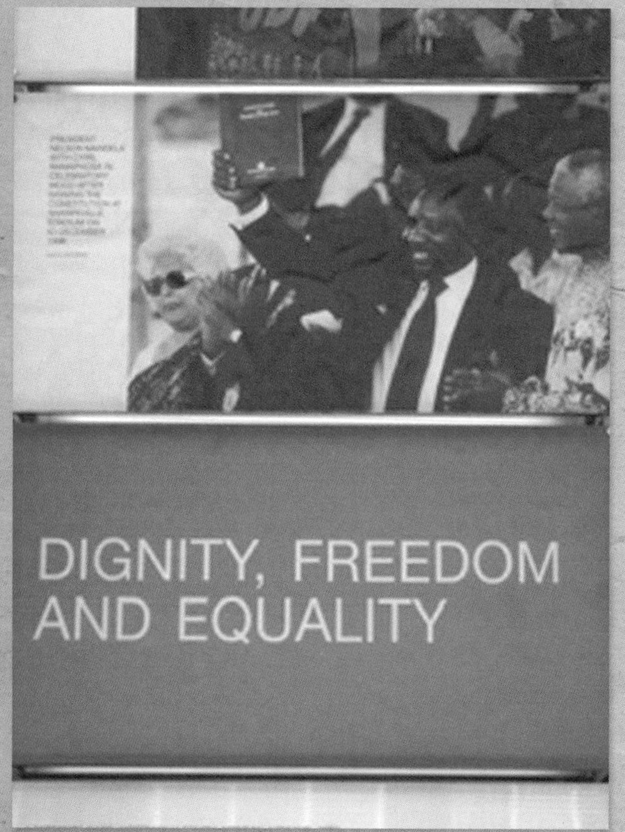

Coming home

should be like returning to a sanctuary.
One you enjoyed creating.
Bring as little baggage home as possible.
Leave your work troubles at the door.

'How can we forget joy?'

I first learnt about **Luis Barragán**, a self-trained Mexican architect, who believed in 'emotional architecture' from an architect friend. He's an architect's architect. 'A work of art reaches perfection when it conveys silent joy and serenity.' His work is simple, yet dense. His exteriors aren't aggressive; they are almost anonymous. He didn't conform. A dreamer at a time when others were embracing International style his work exemplifies solitude; yet he wanted others to see the stamp of his experiences. He found compatability in the villages of North Africa, Morocco, the Greek Aegean, Andalusia and Mexico and used it in a rare way. His houses integrate the garden and follow the natural route in materials, stone or wood. He combined them with a brilliant use of colour and light. It's as if his buildings say hesitation leads to nothing. They are unique and confident, with an element of mystery and surprise. His work expresses his own being; there's a feeling of seclusion. Barragán believed in his emotional and intuitive capacity and explored feelings from an inner life. His understanding of aesthetics was subject to influences: race, origins, customs and history. It allowed him to work with landscape and object design as well as architecture. Little wonder he's a favourite one.

‘Lately I have been thinking how comfort is perhaps the greatest luxury.’

Billy Baldwin, American interior designer

Comfort is not just our physical wellbeing. It’s a state of mind.
Buddhists believe the resting place of the mind is the heart.
The mind is busy listening all day when all it wants is quiet.
The only place the mind will find final peace is inside the silence of the heart.

HOME

You leave the house but come back home

There's no place like it. Your spirit should be lifted every time you arrive home. Otherwise it's just a shelter. Your kingdom should be filled with things that bring you joy and nourish your soul with an atmosphere of appreciation for all that's good in your life. Surrounding yourself with your own traditions feeds your mind.

My sense of home came from my mother.
She did good home.
It always felt comfortable, looked good and all were welcome.
She encouraged friends of all ages.
It was a place to be shared.

So much so that for my fifteenth birthday I was allowed to do up my room as I wanted it. She would 'stay out of it'. Believing this would be a good way to encourage my skills I was let loose. I painted the walls a deep, but at the same time vibrant, green, used Marrimekko cotton in red and pink on the bed and windows, lost the carpet and polished the floorboards. It was suddenly mine. All mine, within the house I shared with everyone else in my family. I learnt two lessons from this present. The first the value of a space of your own and the other that I was able to create an atmosphere that felt like me and no one else.

Discovering your colour palette and expressing it is great fun. Finding colours you feel comfortable with, and getting to know what they work well with, forms a framework that becomes the basis for mixing your pieces. Choosing colours for your home is just like choosing the colour of your clothes. Have fun. Both should feel spontaneous and just like you.

A place or an idea?

The iconic architect Le Corbusier believed 'A house is a machine for living in. An armchair a machine for sitting in and so on.' While he may be right practically speaking, there's more to it than that. The notion of home is primal and domestic wellbeing is a fundamental human need, deeply rooted in us. But domesticity has only existed for about three hundred and fifty or so years and styles of decoration have changed, in size as well as function. For instance Art Deco lasted less than a decade and Art Nouveau barely more than a decade.

Changes in style are primarily a product of fashion and have a lot to answer for. Fashion reinvents itself seasonally which is much more often than changes in human behaviour come about. Use the mantra: I will follow my instincts and won't give in to trends. Seek out true and timeless beauty, based on your own style, as it will far outlast anything else. Trusting your senses and your idea of comfort will help create a haven for yourself and those you want to share it with. By giving your home a personal feel it will never be in or out of fashion. Playing with it and getting it just right can help satisfy your desire for intimacy and hominess.

Tune in to your emotional response when deciding what things you want to live with. Be aware that colour affects your mood. As will the tactility of things. Make your home your retreat. One in which art and beauty have a place and invite contemplation. Appreciate there is beauty in things imperfect, modest and humble. In the unconventional.

Tread lightly. Take a lead from buildings that use sustainable materials as their driving force. Think small, avoid big. Recycle. Love the old and give it new life. Choose pieces that support those in need, the handmade. Special pieces bought while travelling provide lasting memories; unlike a photograph they can be used everyday. Pieces that speak of tradition and about the culture they represent are resistant to fashion.

After all, a cultural identity is important and indigenous architecture makes sense. It's part of what

makes us individual. Homes need to be climate specific too. Lessons are there for the taking from houses that have stood the test of time. Wide verandahs and corrugated iron rooves suit Australia. An Islamic courtyard can be paradise. Adobe houses in the Atlas Mountains blend well with their environment and are naturally cool.

Little things count.

The life in your home is in the detail. Your detail. Nothing is insignificant. Don't be afraid to be eclectic and attend to the small things. Add colour. Your colour. Tell your story using timeless principles. Mixing old and new, rough and smooth tells the story of your life. Have the courage to create something with a personality all its own. Mix things up. Good design is tolerant. Things designed long ago mix well with new pieces. Timeless things go on working, don't draw attention to themselves and are beautiful tools in the more complete picture. Avoid the mass produced. Bland things are a bad use of your natural language.

Layering your home with bits that have age means you are connected to other lives and other times. This is especially true of things that have been a part of your family. You are continuing a story. Valuing them, and caring for them, gives you a connection. Homes layered with things that hold memories tell stories, so I don't understand why some people think of layering in a derogatory way. Perhaps they have no pleasant memories they want to stay in touch with?

Life's a dance between the big picture and the small.

Make a home, don't just live in a house. Most importantly let your home evolve and grow as you do, change it as your life and needs change. The way your home works should reflect your behaviour and consider the comfort of others. Build it around your habits. When the balance is right your home feels like an extension of your soul.

Sharing openly leads to understanding and appreciation

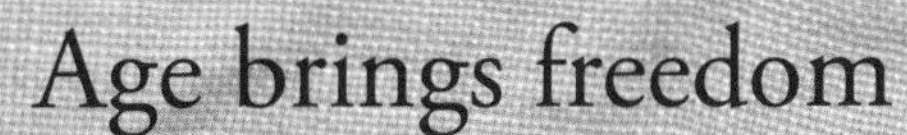

Age brings freedom

apart

People thrive when lives are connected. 'It takes a village to raise a child' is an African saying that brings this thought home.

Typical village life, with communal buildings, a square or green, and self-sufficiency means people need to rely on one another for help. There's a need to share, food is grown and often cooked collectively. Often there's no other way of surviving.

In our heavily populated and fragmented cities we have created new traditions and boundaries, making life more complex. People tend to mind their own business, act with self-interest and self-imposed constraints. We're busy getting on with their own lives so it's easy to forget the village mentality.

Isn't it time we noticed the village lesson, simplified things, connected, and tended to each other's needs?

together

The staff who work in the game parks of Africa live in very close proximity to, and need to rely on, each other for everything, including their safety. More often than not they don't know each other before they begin living together. Miles from anywhere there's no getting away.

All along the dirt highway these communities of nurturers live in simple housing with shared open-air living rooms. Brought together by their love of space and wildlife, many say the greatest luxury they can have is a hot bath. They'll travel miles for one. You get the feeling they value the little things.

Like many other village compounds, with their thatched grass roofs, open-air kitchens and central well, these communities are alive with tradition. Traditions that are well worth keeping. They're the good things that have worked well from the start.

They are great examples of tolerance, understanding the concept of nurturing and sharing, and how we can benefit from it.

A house that contains no sign of the individual who lives there is not a home

Solitary space

It's important to have a place to shut out the world and its demands. Personal space, ideally not your bedroom. Another place to collect your thoughts, somewhere you can think, relax, be honest with yourself; feel tranquil when needed, and stimulated when not. Somewhere, however small, that gives you a sense of solitude and can be a sanctuary for your private thoughts. Visitors need not be welcomed.

This life is full of opportunities and options, accompanied by moments of joy, sorrow, pleasure, and stress. It's not always easy balancing work and home, even harder with a family. We need to find peace amongst daily distractions to be able to thrive and remain balanced. It's easy to lose your way, and with it the ability to totally relax and refresh yourself — body and spirit. Especially when you're a single parent. You won't be the only one who'll reap the benefits, nurturing yourself is a good example to your children. To give yourself the gift of time and space is to nurture your family, your relationships, your career and your passions. You will return to the people in your life refreshed. They too need time out from you.

It seems men have a good understanding of this need, making space for sport, woodworking, tinkering with cars, caravans and boats. For women the message has become not only can we have it all but why not? We feel responsible for making our environments complete and often forget to make space just for ourselves.

My priority has always been my children and with a husband who travelled extensively there were periods when I experienced a loss of private time and space. I longed for a room of my own. I've now claimed some as my children have moved out. I use it all, regularly.

Don't make solitude a wish, make it happen.

White designer
cubes for living
are boring.
Give me creative
layering anytime.
I dream of designer
labels being
ignored and people
worshipping things
that have been
handmade.

I had the house to myself last night. It was great — some precious time alone.

Decisions, decisions, decisions.

Decisions can, at times, feel overwhelming. There's no denying decision making is easier for some than others. We all know decisive people and how they get things done.

The reality is that, once made, a decision means you can get on with that something that you were undecided about.

If your decision is wrong it simply means you can correct it with another.

What's so bad about that?

Or don't you like being wrong?

The other choice is to stay stuck.

At some time we're all guilty of trying not to respond emotionally to situations so we don't appear vulnerable. This is especially true at work …

'Do I call or don't I? I want the job.'

For heaven's sake, how else will they know how badly you want the job? Nothing ventured, nothing gained. It's almost certain the employer will want the keen one.

Decisions, or making a choice, tell us as much about ourselves as our talents do. Cultivating the power to select your thoughts will enable you to make more right choices. Altering the way you look at things, the way you act, means the end result will be clearer.

Decisions are best made.

Not procrastinated about.

They have their rewards.

Hearing his neighbour cry, a little boy went into the old man's garden, climbed onto his lap, and just sat there. When his mother asked what he had said to the neighbour, the little boy replied, 'Nothing, I just helped him cry.'

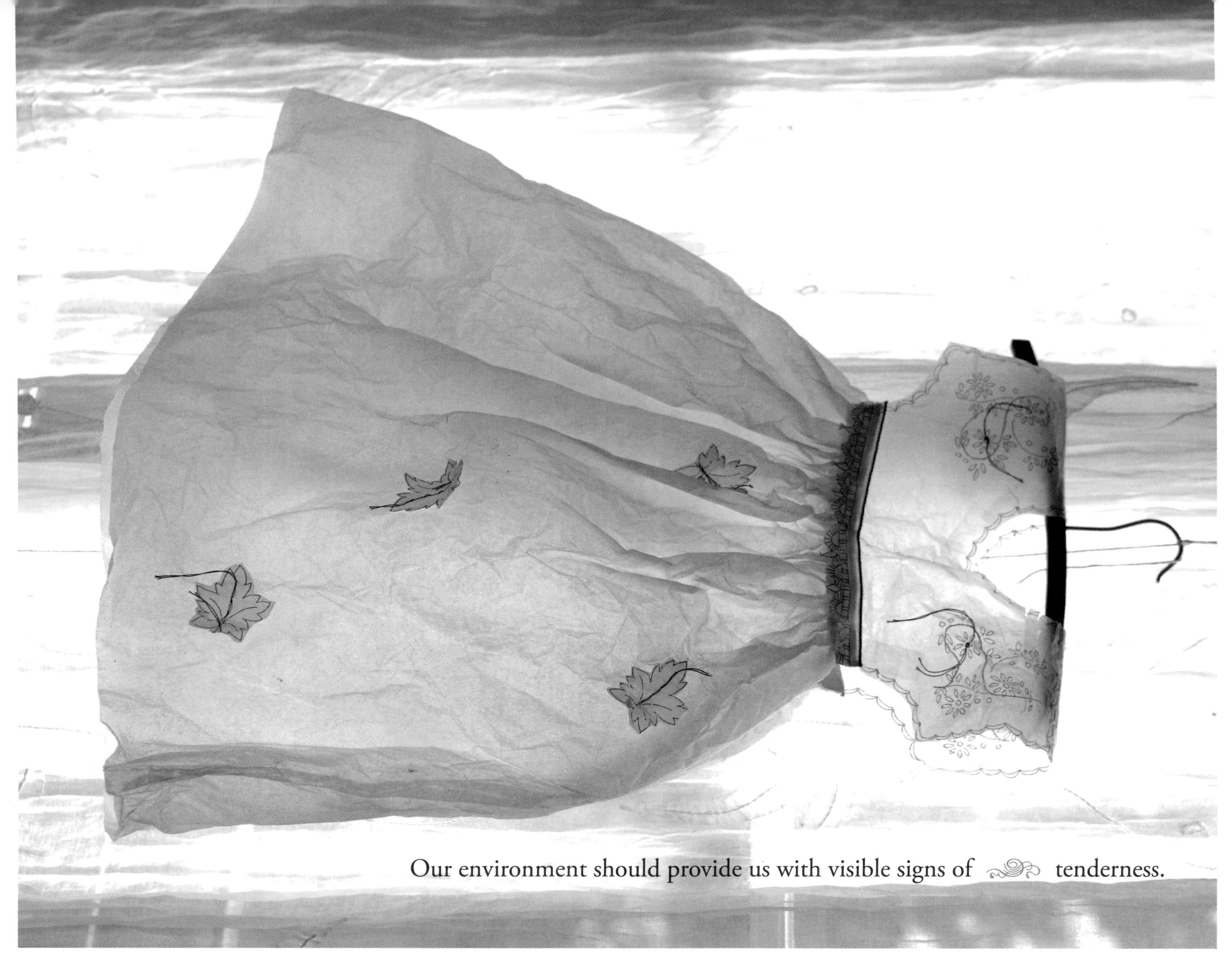

Our environment should provide us with visible signs of tenderness.

To appreciate what's new and different
we first need to appreciate sameness

Different can be unsettling and scary,
but it also holds the seeds for our growth

Some people enjoy living alone.
They don't want to ever
come home from
work again to be asked

What's for dinner tonight?

They go out for that.
It's their choice not to look
after anyone else.
They don't want to have to pick up
someone else's dirty underwear.
The number who feel this way is on the increase.

Count me in

me: 'I'd like to order a dinner hamper for three for tomorrow night please.'
the caterer: 'We only do hampers for two so that means you will need two hampers.'
me: 'Oh. We'll have one too many servings.'
the caterer: 'That's right, but we don't make alterations to our packs or do them for one.'
me: 'There's no way you can?'
the caterer: 'No. So I'll order two for you, right?'
me: 'I suppose so. Thank you. Could I please check what we'll be getting?'
the caterer: 'A steak, sausages, a chicken skewer and salad.'
me: 'We are watching our weight so would it be possible to do them without the sausages please?'
the caterer: 'Yes sure. That will be $10 less each. So less $40 altogether.'

me: 'Oh. So you can change the contents and the price but you can't make a hamper for one?'

BEFORE

AFTER

STREET VIEW OF THE BATHERS PAVILION

BEFORE

AFTER

BEACH VIEW OF THE BATHERS PAVILION

The power of one.

once one is one, no more, no less.

I started a restaurant and café, The Bathers' Pavilion in the old bathing pavilion on the beach at Balmoral, in Sydney. When I arrived in 1988 the building was desperately in need of repair and restoration. As the lessee repairs were my responsibility.

This much-loved public building had a Preservation Order placed on it, which meant any proposed changes to the structure or use had to be approved by two bodies — the local council and the Heritage Council. I put together what I thought was a sympathetic and sensitive proposal for restoration and new use which included a restaurant downstairs (where one had existed for many years) and a small boutique hotel to occupy the unused floor upstairs and approached council for permission to proceed with my plans.

The local council responded positively to the proposal but a small group of residents did not and what followed was a protracted, and expensive, process that regularly filled the local newspaper, the subject of more local council meetings than I care to remember, and a matter that went before the Land and Environment Court four times. It almost had its own act of parliament.

I wanted to preserve and restore the building. It was a project that demanded much of my time and it was difficult to find a balance between building plans, the running of a busy and popular restaurant, being a mother and a wife and support to my husband.

The battle had been raging for about nine years or so when one day a very tall man, who drives a very small car, an old Fiat Bambino, walked into my office with the assurance of someone who understood success. As he sat in my office, he looked me in the eye and asked 'Who's supporting you?' He went on to say that for years he had read a great deal about what a few people didn't want to happen to the building, but nothing about what a lot of people did.

He said that he intended to do something about trying to get another point of view into the public arena. What struck me was how simplistic his idea of turning something negative into a positive appeared. True to his word, he gathered together other like-minded people and placed a full-page advertisement in the local newspaper explaining their point of view and asked other people who shared their view to stand up and be counted by showing their support and writing letters to council.

The response was overwhelming. In a very short time he accomplished what he had set out to do. One person encouraged many other silent people and together they put a balance back into the public discussion.

To me he was a godsend. I named a cocktail after him. I don't know if it's still on the list. He certainly is firmly on mine, and always will be.

People will forget what you said.
They'll forget what you did.
But they'll never forget how
you made them feel.

There should be more afternoons like this

More people live alone than ever before

Communities are changing. Before the Industrial Revolution social life revolved around family and the church. We now live longer and have more free time, plus more choice about how to spend it. Free to discard what we don't want, these expanding options mean social interaction is changing.

Working from home is an everyday thing. Hot desks have been introduced in the interests of efficiency, not to build loyalty. Changed working habits and a shift in spirituality means we have to look elsewhere for a connection that once would have been found at work or the church. Our neighbourhoods are also constructed differently. The most densely populated areas are those where singles live. Leaving a home office to seek out company brings streets alive with cafes, a new kind of church hall. Full with people talking and exchanging ideas.

Some people love their own space, enough to maintain it, to metaphorically stay put within their own four walls, even if they're in a loving relationship. Used to their own space and place, they value it, and it suits them not to have to look after one another's domestics and maintain their independence. They're together but separate, they date and appreciate each other without having to deal with everyday annoyances. Kant, the philosopher, seemed to understand this with his theory that every rational being exists as an end in themselves and that boundaries are necessary to feel emotionally safe.

Belonging

Identifying with our surroundings can be as simple as finding a bookshop we love, a deli where they care enough to know your name and ask about your day, or where transport works perfectly for you. Bonding isn't dependent on structure, form, or the setting, but on emotion, attitude, understanding and perceptions. Shared territory alone doesn't make a community; it involves personal investment.

Good neighbourhood relationships make all the difference. Small daily exchanges. Who wouldn't love a shopkeeper just around the corner who is willing to return mistaken purchases with a smile? One who wastes opportunities, serves you rudely, or worse, plays the ignoring game, is missing the point entirely. They're to be avoided, not you. Small business is a foundation from which daily goodness can spread. As is open space with somewhere to sit and meet those who live around you. A playground shared by all.

Our choice of where we live is in part financial and depends on a sense of belonging. We like to feel similar to those around us. We rely on people around us for a sense of belonging.

It's all about treating other people as you would like to be treated. Shared living, in a block of flats, has its own unique sense of community and the potential to be valuable and supportive. It's a kind of village life, sharing simple everyday things.

It's desirable to feel part of a dependable and stable environment. There's a gift to be had in ordinary everyday things.

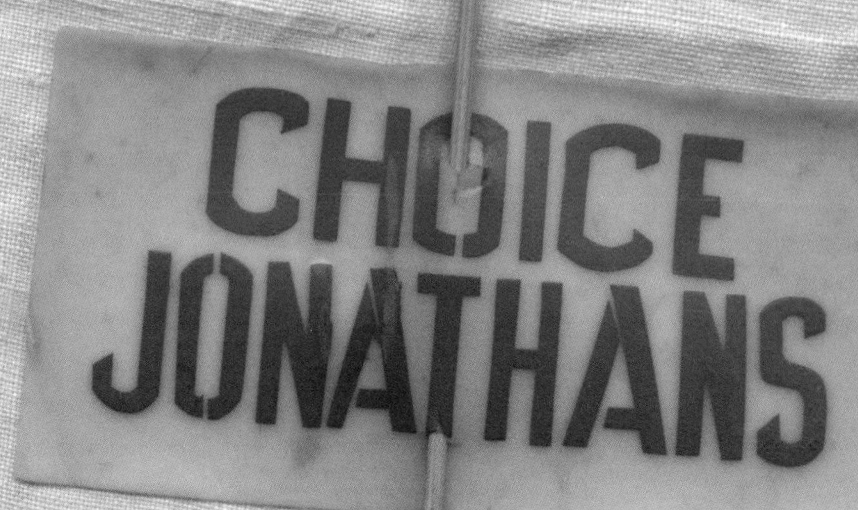

Have you found anyone yet?

It's as if there's a lost and
found department for lovers.

Please
drop the single supplement.
Charge for a room. Same room, same price.
Single and supplement are not meant to be together.

Make sympathetic, smaller packaging.
All the world's a family. But we don't all live together.

Don't say 'are you just on your own?'
Just? Think what the just might make a one feel.

Include ones in anything and everything you would friends who are couples. Ones have just as much to offer.

Drop automatically putting partner on invitations.
If you don't know the person you are sending the invitation to well enough to know the name of their partner, please don't assume they have one. They may want one and it just heightens that sense of being in a minority.

Don't put any unrequested mailers in our letterboxes or better still don't assume every house has more then one person living in it.

Make an ad that looks like someone is living happily on their own. Many are.

Package special holidays and airfares for one.

Inspire other people by acting as if all the world's not a couple or a happy little margarine family.

One in three
break bread everyday,
eat out,
travel,
and don't want to be
regarded as different.

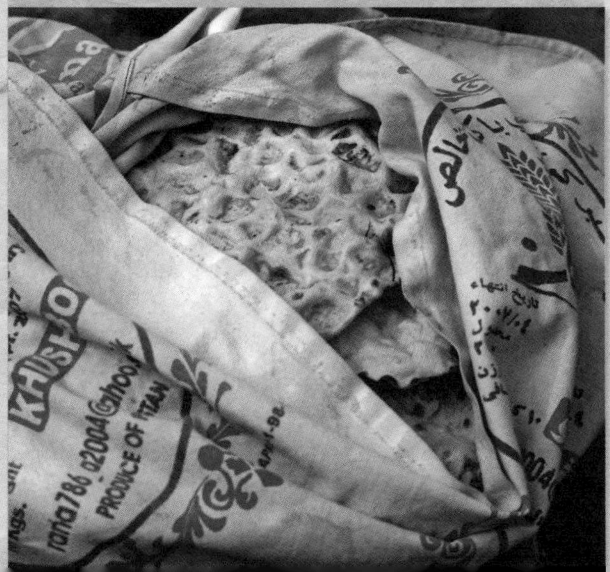

'The ...'

Have you ever noticed when someone starts a new relationship how they refer to the new person in their life as 'the architect', 'the one from the other night' or 'that Swedish girl'? The same goes for professional and personal relationships.
When a relationship moves on into the next stage a new friend is given their name. The architect becomes Cosimo or Paul and so on.
It's all a matter of trust.
Then it begins all over again.
Differently.
Notice how 'the' becomes 'my'?
'My client', 'my friend', 'my boyfriend', 'my special friend', 'my partner, 'my husband', 'my wife.'

Read between the lines.
Not everything is expressed on the surface.

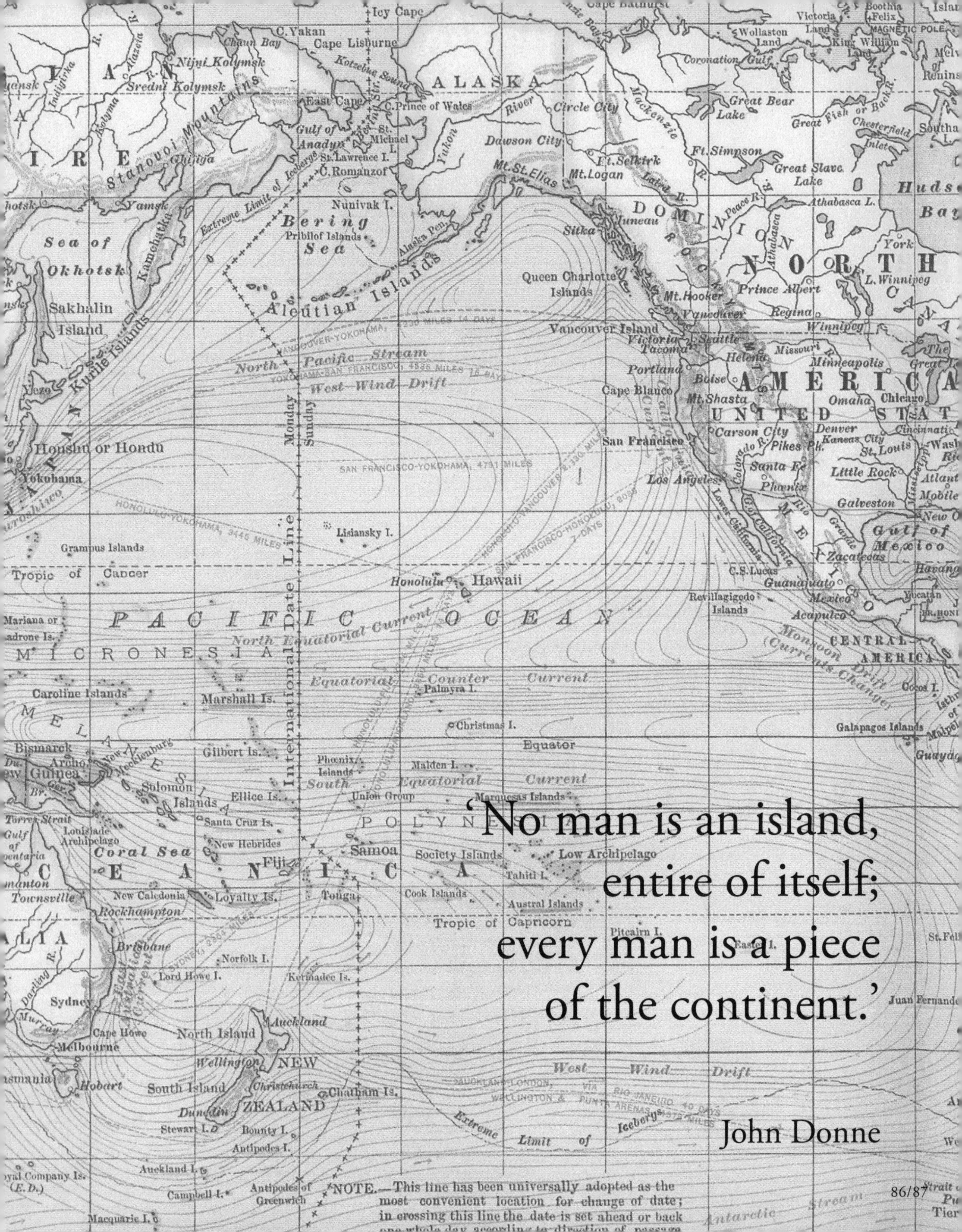

'No man is an island,
entire of itself;
every man is a piece
of the continent.'

John Donne

You may be familiar with Shakespeare's
'To thine own self be true'
But there's more to life.

Keep in mind you are the best judge of what you want,
and don't forget good judges think twice.
Your right to self respect comes from being a human being.
Don't take it for granted. Enjoy it.

Being you is the only thing at which you will always be the best in the world.

You will always know more about what you're thinking about than anyone else.
You always look better than you think you do in the mirror.
The face you see will be far less warm and attractive than the face seen by a friend.
Expressions make faces.
If you do badly at something, and the result is not what you wanted, remember it was only your performance on the day.
The winner one day may not be the winner another.
Never let anyone write you off.
And never, never write yourself off.

The most mundane things can be beautiful

Village people

I feel I live in a village. This happy notion was confirmed when the small, local pharmacy closed for renovations, leaving a handwritten note on the door apologising for the inconvenience which would last only a few days, and informing those of us with prescriptions they kept on file that they were available from the franchised post office across the road. A friendlier post office does not exist. They dispensed the prescription paperwork with warmth and caring despite a total lack of financial gain for them in this extra demand. It's the kind of sharing, caring, feel good stuff that stays with you and keeps you loyal. An act that makes you feel valued as a one and part of something bigger than just you. The complete opposite of an ad campaign for a store that encouraged people disillusioned with life to make a fresh start as a one. Their idea was to buy lots of their furniture and knick knacks in the process. It played on people's emotions by urging them to fill the gaps in their lives with consumables. It's clear who would gain. The store. Unlike the act of kindness demonstrated by the busy people in the post office — where the community benefited. With global brands, and malls with parking lots big enough to lose your car in, gaining the major share of the market let's nurture and protect independent shops and markets run by people who care to know you and treat you as an individual. It will enrich our daily lives in small ways.

Talk
Don’t type

What's mine is mine,
What's yours is mine.

Where's the balance in a relationship when the term 'attached' is used?

It's circumstantial

The right thing for me may be the wrong thing for you. What's right for me today may be different from what's right for me tomorrow.

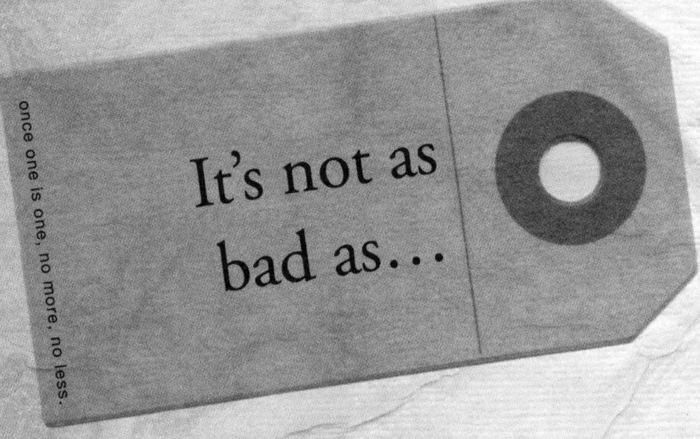

I use 'this isn't as bad as boarding school' as a mantra to remind myself I'm resilient and that whatever I, or my family, are going through will end.

I suffered from homesickness, and a feeling of displacement and loss of identity, during my five years in a country boarding school. Locked away from my family and home meant I was unable to act like the individual I'd been encouraged to be. We were expected to conform. It also meant a lack of privacy. Frozen in bed at night from loneliness and the cold I learnt to feel inferior as my self confidence became eroded. In short I hated it.

It was a long way from home and bore no resemblance to one. Despite the photographs and decorative touches I added to my small allocated space, there was little comfort.

I didn't yet know the importance of being, or how to be, my own friend.

The explanation I was given for being sent to boarding school was my own shyness — my parents felt it would help me find my own voice.

During my final year my parents were called in to see the headmistress because I had been caught talking in class and was accused of being a disruptive influence. My mother rejoiced, I had found my voice. It was comforting to learn that the majority of my much loved book club, all well rounded women who have achieved success, were also products of boarding schools.

Looking back I thought I needed my parents and family support to be able to flourish. Using the experience as part of my resilience plan I now see it helped form the strength I call on during bad times.

I remember reading *The Diary of A Young Girl* by **Anne Frank** while locked in boarding school and her words felt poignant and powerful. Anne was born in 1929 into an upper class Jewish family in Germany. She had no control over the circumstances that lead her to become the author of a diary that's been translated into sixty-seven languages and sold over twenty-five million copies worldwide.

'Despite everything I believe people are good at heart.'

Anne's a favourite one because she couldn't help but see that somehow things would change for the better. Locked away at thirteen, during the Second World War, in a secret, cramped and damp annexe in Amsterdam with her family, and that of her father's business partners, she survived a confined and monotonous twenty-five months by writing short stories, fairy tales and keeping her diary while trying to continue her eduction. She wanted to become a writer or journalist after the war. The family needed to stay silent during the day because noise would have given their presence away to those working below, and they relied on the help of four trusted friends for food and news of the outside world. These were friends we'd all love to have; they risked their lives as the penalty for anyone caught helping Jews was death. Anne heard on the radio that after the war diaries would be collected as a record of what had happened to people so she edited out anything too personal.

On 4 August 1944 the annexe was raided by Nazis and the Frank family were deported to Auschwitz. Anne, her mother and sister Margot, were separated from her father and believed he died. The four helpful friends were arrested but released. Two returned to the annexe, found Anne's writings and kept them safe. Seven months after capture Anne and Margot were moved to a concentration camp separate from their mother. Anne died, at just fifteen, of typhoid, nine months after her arrest. Her mother and sister died too. Her father, Otto, survived, arranged for publication of Anne's diary and with the proceeds set up a charitable foundation to help pay for the medical expenses of Christians who helped Jews during the war.

The ingredients for loving yourself

are the same as for
loving another.
Kindness.
Respect.
Tolerance.
Patience.
Understanding.

People used to stay together for the children.

Sometimes unhappily.

It seemed nobody was single.

Everybody knew a matchmaker without a computer.

God forbid a woman of a certain age who was single.

People would ask, 'What's the matter with her?'

Now if you're twenty-five and single you're simply single.

If you're thirty-five or over, you're single with an explanation.

Like the airlines, dating has been deregulated, with similar results.

It's a different marketplace.

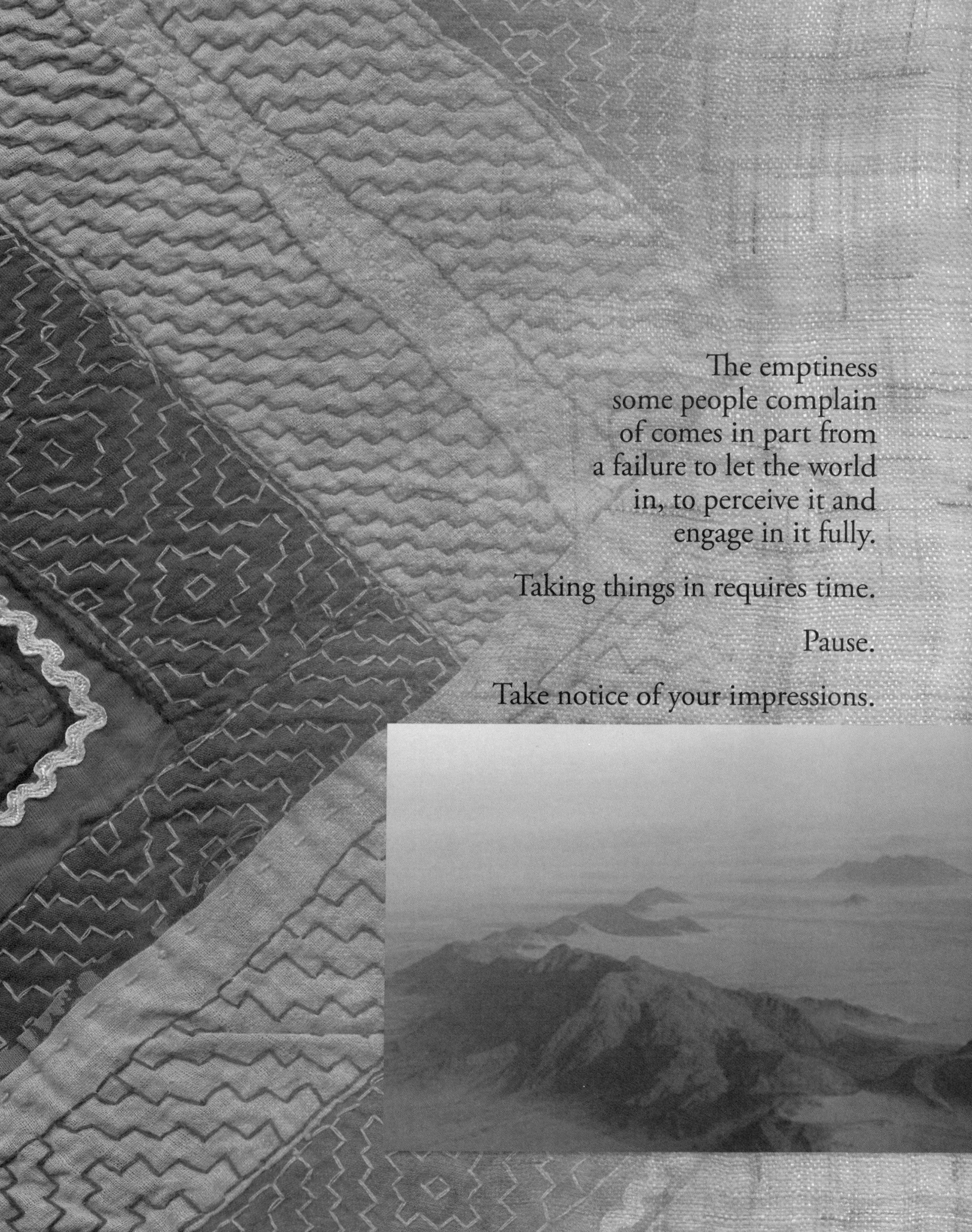

The emptiness
some people complain
of comes in part from
a failure to let the world
in, to perceive it and
engage in it fully.

Taking things in requires time.

Pause.

Take notice of your impressions.

WHEN STARTING TO WRITE THIS BOOK a number of people asked if I was going to include a piece on depression. They seemed to assume I would if I was writing about living alone and being one. I am not a psychiatrist, nor have I trained as a counsellor but I do know from experience that depression is a fact of life. Someone is lying if they say they have never felt a touch of it at some time or other and don't expect to. I also know it feels good to get on top of it; to feel love and support from friends. Accepting help is the best antidote.

If you ask yourself depressing questions, expect depressing answers. It won't do you any good to ask yourself 'Why didn't I?','What if?' or 'Why me?' How would you respond if you were listening to someone else? Swap them for something with a positive answer. Something like 'What can I do to move forward?', 'How can I grow from this challenge?' or 'What can I change to make things better?' It will help you to be resilient and bounce back.

Learn to **forgive.** It just seems stupid not to. Besides, it can tie you in knots.

‘The unexamined life is not worth living.’

The Greek philosopher Socrates (469 – 399 BCE) said way back then that we should look at ourselves. He also said ‘Be as you wish to seem’ which, for a man who said he knew nothing, seems sage advice.

‘I believe that to have world peace we must first have inner peace. Those who are naturally serene, at peace with themselves, will be open toward others. I think this is where the very foundation of universal peace lies.’

His Holiness the 14th Dalai Lama

‘When we respect the natural
cycles of life,
we find that each of
life’s stages has a spiritual
dimension.’

Jack Kornfield

hope for the best

simplify your life
stay motivated
and productive

learn how to be disciplined
and stay focused

sometimes
do nothing

avoid materialism
find happiness in the simple things

start an exercise habit

carry on traditions or start one

enjoy life

Don't let your ex dictate the rest of your life or how you feel about yourself.

I hate the word ex. When you have children and divorce there's no ex about it. You still care. You have to as you both have the responsibility to care for your children — emotionally as well as physically. You may not want to be in contact with each other but need to be, especially when the children are young. For their sake it's best if you find a way to communicate without conflict, then everyone benefits. If you can't do it every day, at the very least express compassion and show love on those special days, birthdays, weddings and funerals.

When the father to my children died I felt like a widow yet I wasn't sure which box I should tick on forms asking for marital status. Divorcee didn't feel right. He was no longer alive and didn't he have to be for me to use that term? Widow wasn't right either as it implied we were married at the time of his death. As a single parent I feel like a widow.

I researched and asked around but there's no term especially for this status of being. I toyed with inventing one — Diwidow maybe. I checked with several government departments and couldn't get a definitive answer as to what I should officially call myself on census forms. 'Was he alive when you divorced him?' one asked. After checking with her supervisor she followed that with 'It's okay to just call yourself whatever it is you feel like.'

So I guess people like me simply become single again. Differently. But this noun still doesn't seem quite right as I have a past and children. That's why I like one.

I knew him.

When Andrew, my children's father, died,
a friend expressed to my middle child
how sad she must be.

The wise one replied
'I was lucky to have known him so well.
Had Mum and Dad not been divorced
I may not have been so lucky.
I will not have to grieve for someone
I did not know.'

Celebrate sadness.
It's okay to feel sad sometimes.
It's a natural response.
Sadness affects the way we think
and thinking involves processing.
To feel a little sad heightens your feelings.
During sad times I've been required to make
some of my biggest decisions, including buying
the home I now enjoy.
Aware it's easy to make a mistake when feeling cloudy
I've had to focus on what it is I really want.
This has meant I've forced myself to think clearly.
It's something I've learnt by my mistakes and
means I'm now less likely to be deceived or
make snap decisions or judgements about people.
Deciding something with an open heart, while
not always easy, usually means making the right choice.

The ripple effect

Seeing someone we love experience a hurt is hard. Sometimes very hard. Being empathetic, the one who listens, their lifeboat, helping them sort out their feelings makes you feel useful. It's a better alternative than feeling helpless. Then there are your feelings to deal with — about how it affects you, your life.

And so, just like them, you need a special someone to talk things through with. An empathetic ear of your own. So the original hurt is layered, it has a ripple effect. It helps to remember ripples come in to shore. They land with a splash, massage the shoreline, and eventually sink into the sand. That is, until the next ripple.

I am not the first woman to look in the mirror
and see her mother looking back.
My mother died too early.
She was in her sixties.
So, as my face becomes more like my
last memory of her I find I miss her more
and realise how young she was when she died.
I'm no longer concerned with how I look or
who is watching.
There are days when I could still cry for her.

Everybody's business
is nobody's business

Look at the world
through your heart
not your head

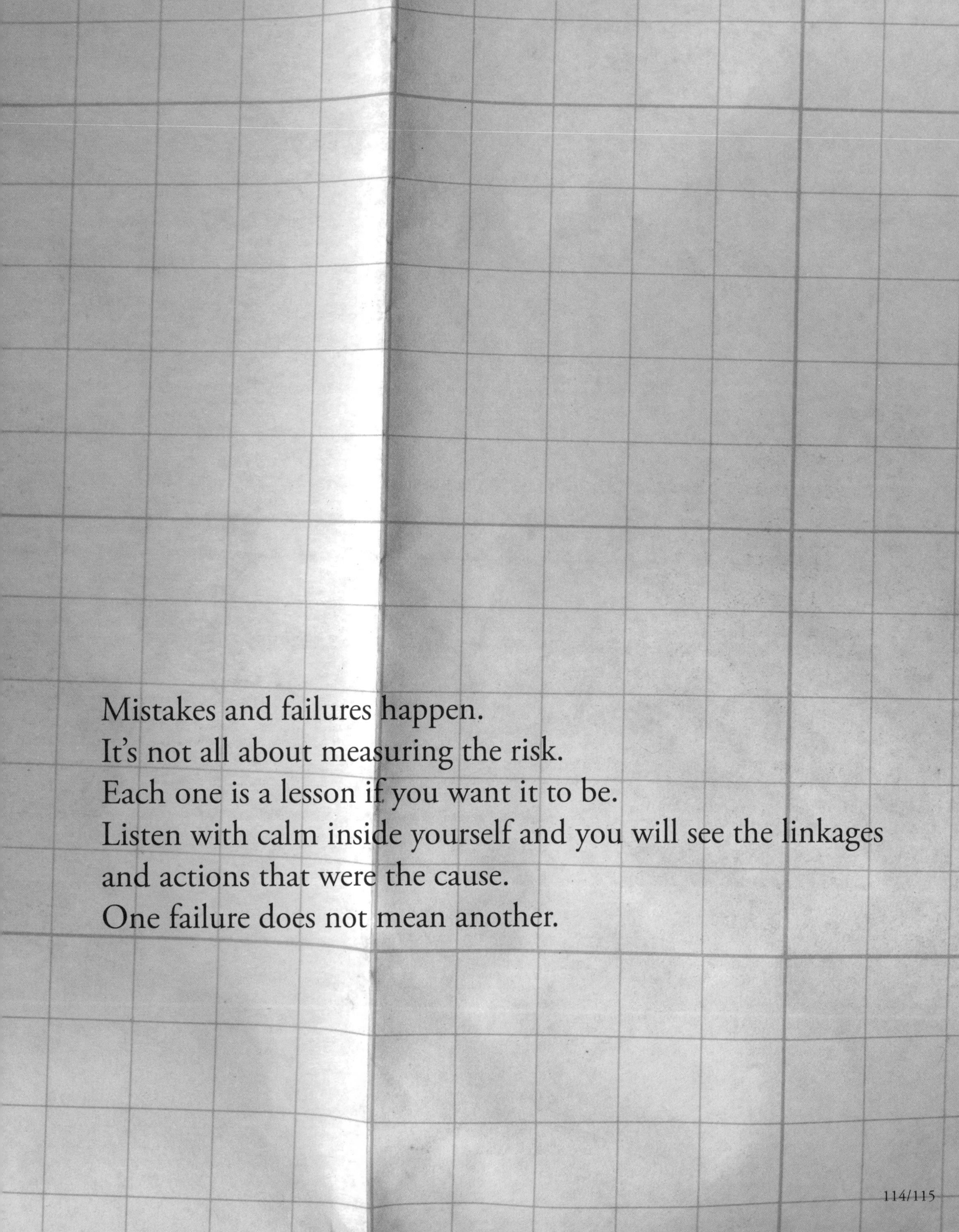

Mistakes and failures happen.
It's not all about measuring the risk.
Each one is a lesson if you want it to be.
Listen with calm inside yourself and you will see the linkages and actions that were the cause.
One failure does not mean another.

Wa is the oldest recorded name for Japan.
But this tiny word is not straightforward.
Scribes used the symbols for balance,
peace and harmony to write the word.
Perhaps this is why we cry 'wa'?

Leave me alone

'Although I am a typical loner in daily life,
my consciousness of belonging to the invisible
community of those who strive for truth,
beauty, and
justice keeps
me from
feeling isolated.'

Einstein

Sometimes we react unpredictably to something someone says.

It may not be the way they say it.

It may be just a single word.

A trigger word.

Like 'fine'.

It's enough to make us all get changed in my family.

Or never cook that dish again.

In some families 'fine' means great.

Just not in mine.

It's all about your language.

And knowing others have theirs.

Many a hurt has gone unnoticed because of it.

Empathetic words create understanding.

Many a heart has been mended because of them.

There's an up side

to being a one.

Flexibility and independence.

There's a little corner shop that sells a mixture of handmade and vintage pieces. The owner previously had a full and busy working life and for years had collected beautiful pieces for the sheer enjoyment of it. There was so much beauty in her life that her husband said she needed to make some space, so she changed direction and began life as a shopkeeper. Two days after she opened he announced he was leaving the seven-year relationship and was going to return to his homeland.

She now finds herself without the support she expected, contemplating divorce, enjoying sharing her things with others.

She feels she and her mother have much in common these days. Her father died four years ago and her mother too became an unexpected one who found her friends wanted to be supportive and tried to include her in things they were doing. She found she has had to explain that now she's a one she has to do the things her husband used to do too and that means there are more demands on her time. She's not so sure they understand.

Death and divorce have much in common. Both involve a period of grieving. The shopkeeper feels the support her mother received is different from the level of support she has experienced since her separation. Some friends are there for her — not all it seems — as her situation can remind them of their own vulnerabilities and make them feel uncomfortable. Divorce is seen as a matter of choice whereas death is not.

Both death and divorce involve an element of wishing for what could have been. They both mean you have to cope on your own and to begin again. In both events the support of family and friends is needed, without judgement. You may be surprised to learn how many people say they have been in a similar situation or know somebody who has. Felt on their own that is.

Why not use every age you are given?

Dirty laundry

Experience has led me to believe things happen for a reason. Ones I haven't always been able to fathom when in the thick of things. But I do know that every time I've made a change it's turned out for the best — or that's how I choose to see it.

I'm not alone in coming to the realisation, all too soon, that there was a problem with my partnership. We had different sensibilities and a different vision and neither of us could find a way through.

Having to say goodbye to a business, one that feels like your baby because you've built it from the ground up, or to a relationship, is difficult indeed. I've started businesses because I've wanted the freedom to make my own decisions, which inevitably includes mistakes, and to try and make a difference in a significant way. I've needed others' faith in me, and have hoped my ideas will succeed. We all seek assurance we belong to something and want our skills appreciated and acknowledged in a meaningful way. To prosper we need the loyalty of others, words of encouragement, and an occasional spontaneous embrace.

It seems when problems arise our outlook narrows and we're not very willing to negotiate or accommodate another persons' point of view.

Other people I've talked to who've also parted from businesses they've started agree it's akin to divorce and different to death. Death is final, while in divorce or the sale of a business the person or thing that you separated from lives on, and can sometimes get in the way. There's no denying both provide strong and rich memories.

With hindsight I've learned the trick is to catch your error before anyone else does. Knowing when to leave or when to stay. The right decision may be to leave, but that doesn't make saying goodbye any easier, especially if you're saying goodbye to someone you love or a business you have created.

With time things look different and it may well be that making your dream a reality was reward enough. Relish the fact your skills, or love, found a useful purpose. You can steer them to success again. Knowing you've acted with integrity and been consistent in your desires makes your decision easier to live with.

Be prepared to change course.

Don't be overwhelmed by your
choices or the lack of them.

Ask yourself
What do I deserve?
Then go about getting it.

We all have a history, some baggage, a past

Just like when you move house, put it in a box,
make sure it's not too heavy,
label it, and store it away.
Safely.
Only to be accessed when useful.

Sometimes it's better not to box it.
Wear it on your sleeve and show the world
you are brave because your mistake taught
you what you didn't already know.
Others may learn from you.

You can always give away what you don't want.
Anytime you choose.

If you care, no matter what the reason, it's simply silly (or rude?) not to call. We all get our wires crossed from time to time.

You may be tied in knots because you're unsure of your feelings. That's understandable. But there wouldn't be a knot if you didn't care. Avoidance is no solution. Try and see it from the other point of view. If someone has taken a risk with you what's the worst thing that can happen if you just get in touch? Honestly. Try it.

The sound of a voice speaks to the heart of things. Picking up the phone can make or change a relationship.

It takes courage to face the source of things said in anger. It makes an honest person out of you.

Everybody has something.

- ☐ I was bullied at school
- ☐ I have financial worries
- ☐ I'm seriously ill
- ☐ There's a serious illness in my family
- ☐ I'm unfulfilled at work
- ☐ I cannot find a job
- ☐ I've been retrenched
- ☐ I don't get on with my boss
- ☐ I hate my office pressures
- ☐ I have unfair demands on my time
- ☐ I'm away from home too often because of work
- ☐ I want a promotion and nobody seems to notice me
- ☐ I cannot find a suitable home
- ☐ The builder is a nightmare
- ☐ I feel misunderstood
- ☐ I'm depressed and don't know why
- ☐ I'm single and would rather not be
- ☐ I've an unfaithful partner
- ☐ I've been unfaithful
- ☐ I'd like a more regular sex life
- ☐ I'm trying to get pregnant but can't
- ☐ I've lost a baby
- ☐ I am dealing with conflict at home
- ☐ My parents divorced
- ☐ I'm divorced
- ☐ I'm widowed
- ☐ My parent died early
- ☐ I'm sad to have had a sibling die
- ☐ I've not had enough sleep
- ☐ I use television as a sedative
- ☐ I wish I was thinner

What's your something?

It's sunny outside ☐
It's raining outside ☐
I have two legs and can walk ☐
I have friends I can talk to at any time of the day ☐
I have a job ☐
I like my job ☐
It's Monday ☐
My family love me ☐
I have two arms to hug with ☐
I have a roof over my head ☐
My clothes smell fresh ☐
I have enough to eat ☐
My home is not being bombed ☐
There's no terrorist at my door ☐
I'm healthy ☐
I have a voice and can use it ☐
My eyes are my window to the world ☐
I've had an education ☐
I can read ☐
There's a library around the corner ☐
I take holidays ☐
I had the place to myself last night ☐
I have a park nearby ☐
I've a friend who was excited to share some news ☐
I have a good relationship with my children ☐
I'm lucky to have my family ☐
I'm not a refugee floating about on a boat ☐
I have a delicious book to read ☐
It's Friday ☐
I slept well last night ☐
I can afford flowers ☐

Don't
STRESS
Find a way to manage it

In 1967 psychiatrists Thomas Holmes and Richard Rahe discovered a correlation between life events and illness and their findings became known as the Holmes and Rahe Stress Scale. By researching the medical histories of five thousand patients they discovered that when our stress levels increase it makes us more susceptible to illness and mental health problems. There's an order to it.

Death of a spouse
Divorce and death of a family member
Injury or illness
Changes at work
Personal injury or illness
Marriage
Retrenched or fired from work; Marital reconciliation; Retirement
Change in health of family member
Pregnancy; Sexual difficulties; Gaining a new family member; Business readjustment
Change in financial state
Change in frequency of arguments
Major mortgage
Foreclosure of mortgage or loan, change in responsibilities at work, child leaving home; trouble with in-laws
Outstanding personal achievement
Spouse starts or stops work; Begin or end school
Change in living conditions
Revision of personal habits
Trouble with your boss; Change in working hours or conditions, residence, school, recreation, religious activities
Change in social activities
Minor mortgage or loan
Change in sleeping habits, number of family reunions, eating patterns
Vacation
Christmas
Minor violation of law

When I first learnt of this scale it helped remind me that others had experienced what I was going through, there would be better and worse things still to come, and to find my perspective in the bigger picture.

We can't avoid stress but we can find effective ways of coping with it to help counteract its negative effects. Being pessimistic, in denial and distancing yourself from stress doesn't solve anything. A positive approach helps to cope with stress — believe there's something you can do to manage your feelings, be gentle with yourself during hard times, accept support from family and friends, especially those who have been through something similar, and talk openly about disappointments. Dealing with things constructively, exercise or yoga, being accepting of stressful circumstances, and remaining optimistic is helpful too.

Be

POSITIVE
Optimistic people live longer

Some people just don't
get it.
They can't.
So let it go.

I first learnt about **Scott Schuman** from my eldest daughter. He's a favourite one, because he seems to understand that

life is way too fascinating to waste time on fashion rules

and much more interesting when people dress in a way that is true to themselves. Scott's created a new respect for street style by sharing his self-taught photography of people on the streets of the world on his blog, www.thesartorialist.blogspot.com, which receives about 250,000 hits each day. His blog has a mix of style, an equality of ages and an understanding of the elements that go into making a look personal. He's great at capturing self-expression.

Shortly after 9/11 Scott decided to change direction. He closed his clothing showroom and began concentrating on his love of photography. He snaps real people, of a wide range of incomes, in real clothes, in real situations, and often posts them without their name or a label — just the place where the photo was taken. He captures someone's personality and acknowledges it as part of their personal style. Some of his subjects share their preferred contacts for essentials such as drycleaning, hair, alterations and shoe repairs.

Scott's photos fascinate me as social documentation of our times. When I travel I too like to snap people in the street. We both encounter language barriers and I get what he means when he says there's a lot in the way people carry themselves. He's able to capture someone's style in a positive, non-judgemental way, is keen to show us his own version of who he thinks each subject is, and for his image to inspire us to create and develop our own style.

Scott says his inspiration comes from contrast and variety. He acknowledges his father as the most influential man in his life. Family values get me every time.

Vietnamese proverb.

I learned an important lesson about trust from a small Vietnamese girl. It was during a trip to Sapa, an old French hill station nestled in the mountains near the Chinese border. It was my second trip to Vietnam and I continued to be amazed by the resilience of the people. Their spirit is infectious. Mostly they are kind, outgoing, welcoming and trusting. Despite their recent history of civil war, invasions by the French, English and the Vietnamese War, which they call the American War, the Vietnamese seem to have the capacity to understand the gentler side of life, beauty, the value of humility, and be appreciating this quieter time in their history. They are also enterprising.

I was travelling with a friend and as we walked into the village early on our first morning we were surrounded by women from nearby hill tribes. Each minority, Flower H'mong, Black H'mong, D'zao, Lao and Red Yeo, was made identifiable by their dress. The women were carrying exquisite textiles made by hand that, just like them, had an open feel. Finding ourselves in the midst of a spontaneous street market it was hard to stop smiling. Many of the pieces were the same, but at the same time entirely different because of the hand that had joined, embroidered or woven them.

The embroidery, hand spun and dyed indigo, fascinated me, as did the reverse appliqué that reveals the bottom layer of colour. One young face shone amongst the ten or so others — Chu was so much smaller, a child among adults. Her eyes sparkled with wisdom beyond her years and her smile came from her soul. She had a single quilt to sell, made by her mother. My friend had meanwhile engaged with an older girl, Khu, and they were talking about serious walking routes. (He's a one. Most definitely a one he would say. He's hiked his way around the world, thinks the Kokoda trail was not the hardest walk he's done, and carries a camera he knows inside out, and he can remember every time they clicked together.)

What followed were some of the most memorable days I have had when travelling. Two girls, who hadn't known each other before now, simultaneously and spontaneously became our guides. We walked kilometres together past and through rice fields, pristine wooded areas and villages where women with blue-stained hands dyed hand spun and woven hemp in pots of boiling indigo, many of which were strung out on poles or across paddocks to dry in the sun. In one village women dressed traditionally in Red Hmong clothes sat in a large circle embroidering and talking. All the women we passed were traditionally and proudly dressed in their minority splendour and looked like walking mosaics.

Khu invited the three of us to her family's simple, mud floor, one-room home for lunch. To get there we passed through rice fields, jumped on stones to cross water courses, and passed her small brother hard at work on the back of the family ox. Alongside the rice, the family grew hemp plants to spin and weave. The house had simple wooden walls that let shafts of light through and a thatched roof. The cooking was done on a small fire in the corner. The bedrolls were rolled up in another corner and there was a single privacy curtain. With no telephone, her mother had been given no warning of our visit but this didn't seem to matter at all. We had picked up some simple provisions on the way and she cooked a very memorable meal in no time. It was while sitting outside under the thatched eaves as we chatted with Khu's sister as she embroidered — eight-year-old Chu acting as interpreter — that I felt a small, warm hand take mine. Chu's hand felt as if it knew the value of work and didn't move again until we left about an hour later.

Khu and my hiking friend walk more quickly and went on ahead and while doing so bonded. As did I with my shorter, smaller, slower walking friend. Chu's story gradually unfolded and I learned she was on school holidays, spoke two languages fluently — Vietnamese and impeccable English. She was proud to tell me she did well at school. She was incredibly trusting, open and had been given the responsibility of selling her mother's quilt to supplement the family's income from their rice paddock and ox. She had walked about ten kilometres into Sapa and was living on her own in a tiny rented room, a long way from home. She didn't ask for anything, had grace and was self-sufficient. Chu also reinforced something I already knew — that age is no barrier to friendship.

I'll never forget the look on her face as she ran across the square on the second morning, or the enveloping warmth of her hug. She was happy we were both where we had agreed to meet. It was as simple as that. Firm arrangements make for firm friendships. She had no watch by which to tell the time and no further plans. Her mother's quilt remained unsold, she was surviving on past sales, and had no expectation that I would be her much needed next customer. We walked and talked and shared some food, met locals and explored the area. She's the best local guide I've ever had.

On the third day Chu wanted me to meet her family so the two of us travelled to her home on the back of an unknown driver's bike. Grateful not to have to walk she was totally relaxed and barely hung on to the driver or me despite the windy dirt road. We got off the bike some way from Chu's home and again walked through villages and across rice paddies to get there. It was another single room, thatched roof, mud floor home — this time there were chickens out the back.

Chu's family were not expecting her and we found her mother and aunt standing knee deep in water planting rice. Her father seemed to be minding her three younger siblings. Nobody seemed particularly surprised to see her beaming face. I was struck by the amount of respect they showed her. I was given a house tour, introduced to the family, shown the chickens and the ox and then Chu discreetly passed over a small roll of notes — the income she had made for them all — along with a thoughtful little gift for each. Then we left, just as we had come, through rice fields and past oxen at work. Our lift was patiently waiting exactly where he said he would be.

Even though she possibly wasn't going to see her family again for weeks Chu showed no signs of resentment or remorse at leaving and having to meet their expectation, that she should continue working during her holiday. It was expected of her and she would happily do it. No, I didn't buy Chu's mother's quilt. I believe she too understood the gift of friendship, some time spent together, some meals shared and knowledge exchanged. I trust someone else is enjoying the quilt.

Leaving Sapa and this warm, emotional connection was a huge tug on my heart. The way Chu ran after the car as we pulled away tells me it was for her too. My friend wondered if Chu was vulnerable and felt concerned that somebody may take advantage of her. I suspect not. I trust her intuition. She is too savvy and astute for that. I often think about her, and have never met anyone else quite like her. I would not be surprised to learn she is running her country in years to come.

Don't pay twice

When you make a bad decision, and you will, accept it. Don't beat up on yourself and pay for it twice.

It's good to put stock
into other people.

It's also worth remembering
stocks rise and fall.

Make sure a wishbone is not where your backbone ought to be.

Sometimes things just don't measure up.

Try adjusting expectations to a realistic level.

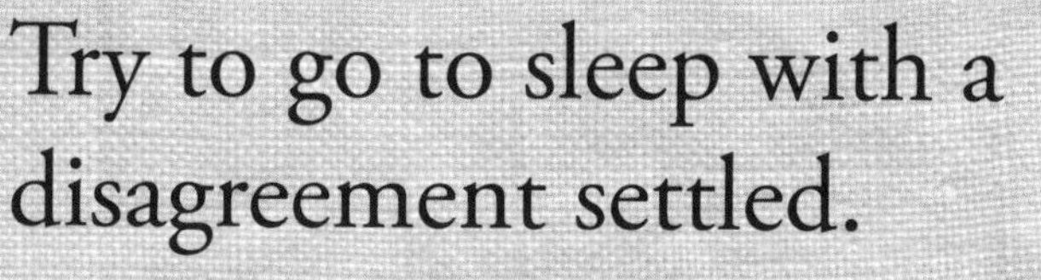

Try to go to sleep with a disagreement settled.

Wake up to a fresh start every morning.

There are times when you hurt.
It's impossible not to.
Knowing the meaning of sorry helps.

Sorry

Not everyone understands its incredible power.

In the middle of a field at a writers' festival,
white tents all around,
just the right amount of sun on my back, feeling luxurious at having
time to sit and listen to the wisdom of others, I heard a clear, warm
young voice read aloud this meaning of sorry.
His words have stayed with me as I imagine
they will with you.
It went like this.

'And it becomes clear to me that it's a good word used by good
people. Nobody is truly virtuous…
But it's good people who can tell the difference, who know when
they've crossed the line.
And it's a hard and humbling gesture,
to take blame and admit fault.
You've got to get brave to say it and mean it. Sorry.
Sorry.
Sorry means you feel the pulse of other people's pain,
as well as your own,
and saying it means you take a share of it.
And so it

binds us together, makes us trodden and sodden as one another.

Sorry is a lot of things.
It's a hole refilled.
A debt repaid.

Sorry is the wake of misdeed.
It's the crippling ripple of consequence.
Sorry is sadness,
just as knowing is sadness.
Sorry is sometimes self-pity.
But Sorry, really, is not about you.
It's theirs to take or leave.
Sorry means you leave yourself open,
to embrace or to ridicule or revenge.
Sorry is a question that begs forgiveness,
because the metronome of a good heart won't
settle until things are set right and true.
Sorry doesn't take things back,
but it pushes things forward.
It bridges the gap.
Sorry is sacrament.
It's an offering.
A gift.
Yes. Sorry is when good people feel bad.'

Craig Silvey grew up on an orchard in Western Australia. The quote you have just read is from his second novel, *Jasper Jones*. He wrote his first at nineteen.

The other side of sorry is forgiveness.
It's liberating.
Healing for the forgiver
and the forgiven.
If you can forgive and
live as if you have forgotten
you will move on.
Moving on leaves space for
other things.
Good things.

There's a being alone

We all need human warmth and connection to

difference in
and lonely

keep us from feeling isolated, separate.

'There is a community of the spirit. Join it, and feel the delight of walking in the noisy street, and *being* the noise.'

Rumi

A gift

Having someone believe in you is a gift. It keeps you honest and helps you reach your potential. I have friends who helped start me on the journey of this book. They're good friends to have.

Each time I came back from a trip I'd email them a few shots I liked of my trip and they'd often respond by saying, 'You should do something with your photographs'. As the same words were repeated by different people who know a good shot from a bad one it made me think, and their words began to resonate.

They really took on meaning after I lost almost all of my photographs when my computer's hard drive imploded. I had back up but, as rarely happens, that failed at the same time. Losing all but a few shots taken over the past five years, and the memories associated with them, felt like losing old friends.

That loss was the catalyst. I decided I should do something with the surviving images. Luckily, friends still had the photographs that I'd sent them and as they emailed them to me and the photographs popped up on my screen I saw the story they told.

They felt familiar, yet new, as if I was seeing them for the first time through someone else's eye.

As I trawled through the images it became obvious there were stories within each. They no longer felt just like a snap I'd taken on a trip. The essence of the people who had generously given me permission to take their photo came back to me and reinforced what I already knew — I knew them as they knew me. We trusted each other. We were one and the same.

At first I was reluctant to change from film to a digital camera. What I didn't understand was that using one would open a different world. You can take a snap, share it, and have an exchange that bypasses language and cultural barriers. Once shared with friends the memories can also come back to you and be put to good use.

Using your intuition is about following your gut feeling, listening to other's advice but following your own — no matter what, trusting your insight and knowledge without using reason or a need to justify. Intuition is not logical, but knowing that following your instincts helps find solutions to problems should be enough to follow its hints, nudges and tuggings.

For Carl Jung, an influential thinker working with opposites, intuition was one of four psychological types. He placed intuition opposite sensation, and feeling opposite to thinking. Jung argued one of these four functions was primary in each person's consciousness and that the opposite function was underdeveloped. I politely disagree. I think for the majority of us, if we take time out, think carefully about our fears, aspirations and instincts and act on them, it's possible to reach decisions that give us a sensational feeling of satisfaction.

Make a promise to yourself to listen to your instincts, follow your gut feelings, and act on them. I hope to never again find myself saying if only …

follow your instincts

Can do

Such a positive sound.
Can do people get it done.
They use their head, heart and hands.
They're practical people. All shapes and sizes.

Here's the thing about them — what they do works.
Watch them work. They make mundane things beautiful.
Their view of the world is one of sharing.

Be a can do one and you'll live a fulfilling life.
One that rises to challenges and reaps the rewards.
Be open and honest.

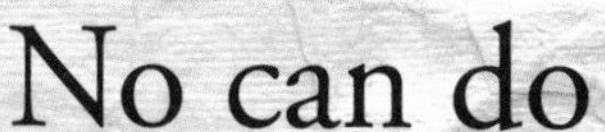

No can do

Such a negative sound.
Can't do people can get you down.
They miss out and those around them do too.

There's this thing about them — they give the
impression life is hard work.
Don't they understand bad times help
us recognise our inner strengths?

With the power to choose happiness for ourselves,
a little nurturing, and understanding
a whole new world is possible.
It involves being open and appreciating what we have.

The Japanese believe
that once touched,
some things take on the soul
of the person who touched them.

'It's us who make the difference.'

Luckily I was given a book called *Banker to the Poor*, which is how I learnt about **Professor Muhammad Yunus**, a favourite one. Born in 1940 in Chittagong, a seaport in Bangladesh, he is the third of fourteen children, five of whom died in infancy. Yunus believes that credit is a fundamental human right, and that instead of business being about everything for its own profit, it should act selflessly and benefit others. During the mid 70s, when famine in all its ugliness was spreading before his eyes, he used his own money, and later went guarantor, for small personal loans to women in Bangladesh. He has helped free thousands from poverty. Before Yunus put his faith in these women only those who had collateral could borrow. By changing the 'silly' rules, and teaching them about finance, the women have learned to manage money themselves. It was revolutionary for women in Bangladesh to be trusted with money.

While teaching economics Yunus questioned the value of economic theories in his efforts to find a solution to poverty. Wishing to 'just be a human being', wanting to stand next to another human being and see if he could touch and help them, this visionary redefined his role and came up with micro-credit. It began with a desire to understand the life of the poor and so he faced reality by visiting the poor households in a nearby village, Jobra, and talking with a woman in desperate need. Sufia Begum, squatting barefoot on hard mud, was making a beautiful stool that was in total contrast to all around her. He learned she earned 50 paisa (US$0.02) a day, and that as she didn't have the 5 taka (US$0.22) to buy the bamboo she had to borrow from the trader to buy it. In return she was forced to sell him her products exclusively and accept the price he offered. Slave labour. Yunus knew that giving her money to avoid the loan shark would be charitable, but would not help in breaking the cycle of poverty, and so made a list of the forty-two people in the village who were borrowing from loan sharks. The total amount owing was US$27. He couldn't believe people had to suffer so much for such a small amount of money.

Yunus believes human beings are essentially good and so his solution was simple. He gave the villagers the US$27 and told them to return it to the loan sharks and be free, no conditions applied.

'If you can make so many people so happy with such a small amount of money why shouldn't you do more of it? So I wanted to do more of it.' He went on to establish the Grameen Bank, a bank devoted to providing the poorest of Bangladesh with minuscule loans. It now provides over 2.5 billion dollars of micro-loans to more than two million families in rural Bangladesh. Without collateral, or lawyers, almost 100 per cent of loans are repaid. Around the world, micro-lending programs inspired by Yunus are blossoming. Grameen has no loan contract, instead it has a social contract, the 'Sixteen Decisions'. These include an undertaking to draw water from a tube-well, to dig a pit latrine, to educate children, and to do no social injustice. Yunus says 'These decisions came out of their own discussions, we didn't impose them … they memorise them, they repeat them, they chant them as slogans.' They're part of their lives. The loan has nothing to do with it, they get the loan anyway to change their lives.

Yunus grew up in a village, which he says encourages imagination as you have to devise your own toys and games. His parents taught him respect for humanity and a powerful sense of purpose. His father finished school at eighth grade, and his mother at fourth grade, but insisted their children were educated. His mother was charitable, the money lender and fixer of the family, whom Yunus ran errands for. Using her example he saw that when money was lent to women the whole family benefited. Not surprisingly he used some of the $1.4 million prize money he and the Grameen Bank received when they won the Nobel Prize in 2006 to create a company to make low-cost, high-nutrition food for the poor, and towards setting up an eye hospital in Bangladesh. His dream is the total eradication of poverty from the world.

Ideas matter more
than things.

Food is the essence of our very existence. It's an ancient craft that's central to any culture. Just as the music we listen to, the books we read and the language we use are. A good meal is probably the most trusted currency in the world so charm yourself with one. Make things with care using fresh ingredients as a way to express the love and respect you feel for yourself. Cook food you know and love when you need comforting.

Old family favourites are nurturing and give the feeling of having family with you without anyone actually being there. Be creative and experiment when you are feeling adventurous and make enough to have some other time. That's what the freezer is for.

Be under no illusion.
It is up to you what you
make of your life.

海

1932

（图名：最新上海地图）

In the past men withdrew to a smoking room.
My how things have changed.

In the words of Picasso **'I am always doing that which I cannot do, in order that I may learn how to do it.'**

Creativity means taking risks,
is inventive and experimental.
Close your eyes, imagine.
See what you come up with.
You're limited only by your imagination.
Imagination leads to inspiration.
So use what you have freely.
And make. To your heart's desire.
Things with your hands, your head and moral choices.
They're all creative acts because
they require risk and courage.
Visualise your actions, imagine the outcome and act.
When you're done don't listen to the judgements of others.
You only have an audience of one to please.
Living a creative life means losing the fear of being wrong.
Creativity brings about change, and to change is to mature,
to mature is to go on creating yourself endlessly.

We all need good friends

Aristotle warned
'The desire for friendship comes quickly.
Friendship does not.'

Some count childhood companions, unlikely allies, chance acquaintances and useful contacts in triple figures on Facebook or Twitter, others only a precious few who they can confide in when they know they are probably at fault, as friends. Friendship is important to a happy life. Lovers come and go, work can carry us halfway around the world, but friendship is a point of stability in an otherwise changing world.

Try to see things from the other person's point of view.

cold hands warm heart

Touch is the first sense to develop when we are born. Our body is the way in which we experience the world. It's the way in which we express empathy, intimacy and affection so it's no small wonder we sometimes long to be touched. Touch calms the mind and soothes the body.

Touching can be a way of demonstrating what you love. Our blood pressure usually lowers when we are touched in a friendly, trusting way. There's an honesty to it. Touch also allows us to make things intuitively — music, art. It's important to know the power of touch.

Feeling connected

To learn, teacher and pupil need to be present.
Both are within us and need to engage if we are to get the lesson.
So it is with relationships.
Reach out and let yourself be touched by others.

'I couldn't feel, so
I tried to touch'.

Leonard Cohen

‘Real knowledge is to know the extent of one’s ignorance.’

Confucius

A natural view of the world

I used to watch nature programs in wonderment with my children. We loved **Sir David Attenborough's** enthusiasm. From the beginning he has talked of the impact humans have made on the natural world, pointing out our destruction of the environment and ways it could be stopped or reversed. Attenborough believes that the future of life on earth depends on whether humans take action. He thinks we need a fundamental change in our societies, economies and politics if we are to have a healthy and habitable planet — something he believes we have a responsibility to leave for future generations of all species.

Despite being rejected for a job as a radio producer, and being told his teeth were too big for television, naturalist Attenborough's career has lasted more than fifty years. He turned down an offer to become Director General of the BBC to record images of natural history. And aren't we glad he did.

He considers overpopulation to be the root cause of many environmental problems and wants us to curb population growth so other species will not be crowded out. He's also concerned the Earth's climate is warming and attributes it to human activity. He feels that in the past we didn't understand the effect of our actions but we no longer have that excuse as we recognise the consequences of our behaviour. Attenborough wants us to act to reform it; individually, collectively, nationally and internationally. Otherwise the future will be a catastrophe. He's supported placing wind turbines in a British 'Area of Outstanding Natural Beauty', arguing we must be prepared to accept the visual effects of something designed to combat climate change.

An agnostic, he believes evolution is an historical fact with evidence all over the planet clearly showing it to be the best way to explain life's diversity. He questions natural selection as the only mechanism and is against globalisation on the basis of economic advantage.

He believes fifty percent, the urbanised half, of the world has lost touch with life's cycle and that those who live in the country have a better understanding of it.

His love of nature began with a childhood rock collection and grew when his adopted Jewish sister gave him a fossil. He doesn't own a car and hates driving, has been voted the most trusted person in Britain and had a species of plants, the *Nepenthes Attenboroughii*, dedicated to him. At 83 he says there's still more to see and do and while his feet are still willing he'll continue to do it. There are very few places he hasn't been. He's been lucky enough to see much of what the world offers. Naturally he's a favourite one.

Nobody's perfect

Celebrities and supermodels take up space showing off their tiniest possible role model bodies. This is nothing to aspire to. Most starve to reshape themselves, are twenty-three percent thinner than the average woman and ninety-five percent of the female population. The high heels they wear may cause arthritis in later life.

When asked, most don't even like their own bodies. That's nothing new. Women generally aren't crazy about theirs and lack a generous spirit towards themselves. A sales driven version of perfection is almost unattainable so it's craziness not to accept size, colour, age, and every detail about ourselves and celebrate our differences instead.

There are no rules for living

All or nothing

once one is one, no more, no less.

Femininism delivered a lot of changes. Living through that time was to live with the firm believers telling — no, convincing — women they could have it all, work with equal opportunity and pay, sex with whoever you wanted and as often as you liked and, if you wanted, a partner to settle down and have children with as well.

There's no denying feminism left us with a new freedom, one we're grateful for. Some would say it's too much as in the aftermath there are many thirty-somethings who feel overwhelmed by their options. Having observed an older generation trying to juggle a full and busy life they have decided to do away with the notion of having it all and concentrate on one aspect of their life, a career or family, while leaving time for themselves.

We've passed on a legacy of what we weren't told — that it's okay to ask for help, to share roles and say no to the parts of life that don't fit with who you want to be. Yes, feminism altered the female role, and hopefully the days of 'I'll ask my husband' are long over, but it seems we don't always know what's good for us. After all, it was a dentist who added sugar to chewing gum in 1869 and he should have known better.

In rejecting the superwoman role, working mothers are confused and bewildered by the complications attached to their choice of priorities. The issue is how to feel useful and fulfilled. As the age of options has emerged so with it has choice and disillusionment. Multitasking works to a degree and can be useful. Except perhaps when using headaches as an excuse not to have sex.

Some mothers feel they are failing by not being involved in their children's school lives, and find not working is no solution. They want to work, to feel useful and needed, and the satisfaction and self-esteem that flows from that. And to contribute to household finances. For many there is no choice.

The secret to achieving an enjoyable life, one that's manageable without being stressful, is in how we manage our time, our demands and what goes on inside our own head. To have the courage to make your dreams come true requires sacrifices along the way.

Contentment can seem hard to achieve when feeling torn in many different directions. At one stage I was managing what felt like five jobs — that of a wife, a mother and homemaker, a restaurateur and a project manager for a complicated

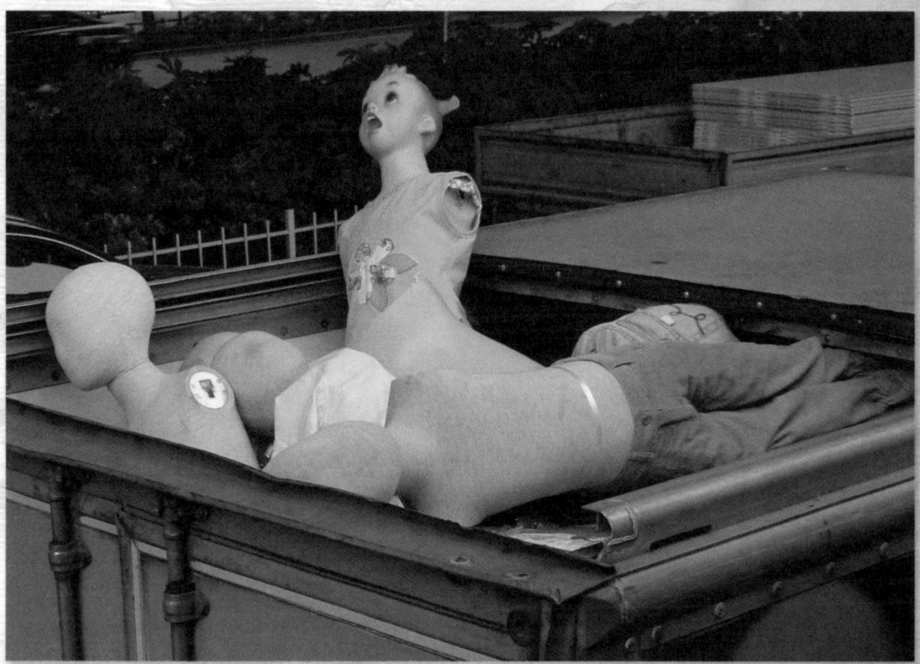

approval process and major refurbishment of a building. The hard part was finding a way to control the balance between being the mother I wanted to be, a social life and work demands. I've always loved my work and felt it is part of the art of who I am. I was happy to choose home life over going out and am not at all regretful of my choice; although sometimes there's a tiny tug of what could have been when I see friends who established relationships through school connections. Working mothers definitely do miss out on this.

I would regularly be asked, 'who's minding your children?' in what felt like a disapproving way. Perhaps sometimes it wasn't and it was my internal guilt at being torn between being at home and work that made it feel that way. Or was it the different reactions I got when I replied either 'their grandmother' or 'our nanny'? Grandmother appeared acceptable, and even elicited a touch of envy once or twice. But the nanny was another matter. The reception was less accommodating. I believe, and my children agree, they were lucky to have learnt to trust and rely on someone else outside our family. They were at home with a trained and devoted person who loved them and who was entirely dedicated to their wellbeing, stimulation and care. They knew they also had a mother and father always interested in them as a priority, ready for a cuddle and pleased to be with them.

When my first daughter was born I was working as a stylist and art director. The flexible nature of freelance work meant that she could come along and now, as an adult, she is following a similar path.

There is no denying that working in my own business meant I was able to drop or defer all else when my children needed me. As an employer I felt the juggling and struggle of others who were not able to be in charge of their time to the same extent. To have a sick child at home when you are at work is to me a version of hell. It's just one of the times when your role as mother can make a difference above all else.

The fact that the majority, if not all, of my income was spent on childcare makes it now seem a ludicrous choice to have made, except for the belief I still hold. That to lead by example is the best thing you can do for your children. My mother didn't work. I was sure my children would need to.

Sharing roles means more couple or solitary time but the blurring of gender roles has confused things. If women understand having it all is impossible but the alternatives remain unclear, how are men to know what fits and what doesn't, what's right and wrong when trying to manage a relationship? In the meantime men have, perhaps a little more quietly, reinvented their rules. It's okay to want to stay at home, not to wear a tie to work, to express emotion, and not to be tied to one job for life. A slower revolution, but just as meaningful in a world where we're supposed to have all the answers, all the time.

Considerable also is the persistent undercurrent that true happiness is only to be found in intimate attachments, especially when it comes to sexual fulfillment.

It's no wonder the expression 'a generation of losers' is entering our vocabulary. Having been set up to believe the unachievable is achievable — to maintain a perfect family and a perfect working life simultaneously — those who feel there is no right path, or that the choices are too many or too hard, are feeling like losers because the guidelines are murky, unclear in their benefits. Financial compensation is not the only measure.

Many in the X and Y generations are choosing to pre-empt failure and complications by deferring marriage and babies. They want to avoid negotiations over how they should live, believe in their natural freedom and can be heard to say they don't intend to get married, or to have children. They feel love and friendship are important, are reluctant to commit, know relationships are not the only source of happiness and see a fulfilling career and living on their own as having it all. They understand there is always an element of uncertainty in any relationship, and that they take work. Nobody should believe anything less. They also don't believe marriage is the principal source of happiness; perhaps fewer will end in tears.

What we all have in common is the drive on one hand for companionship, love and all that goes with it and on the other, the drive for independence, separateness and autonomy. Understandable for both sexes is that the struggle of balancing time, energy, and love between home, work and nurturing ourselves is nothing less than demanding. We can all name people whose lives have been made worthwhile by their work, whether or not their relationships were good or not. Evidence of the attraction in leaving the trace of a life made worthwhile by work is clear. It's about fulfilling a function and that function involves justification of our existence.

Perhaps it was simpler when there were fewer options. While men worked, women filled the homemaking roles. Everyone was clear what was expected of them. Until the children left home. People with no interests other than their family sometimes felt intellectually limited. The reverse is not true of those who work and have no family.

None of this is easy. We all have the gift of our own free will. Rarely does life give us exactly what we want. It is what it is. We are the way we are. Our most significant moments are when we gain new insight and feel personally integrated and content. Without self-respect, a lack of caring about what others think, the support of those who love us and allowing ourselves to sometimes fail, there is no liberation.

Let's rejoice that things have come a long way, on the back of feminism and with the help of technology we are now able to work from home, making sea and tree changes possible. Our interest in sustainability has increased and we now plant community gardens, have chickens in our backyards and share produce with our neighbours. Who knows where this will lead but we have to remain hopeful that any change will consider the past and grow from it.

Lead by example. Show others what can be achieved.

'It's very you.'

Find your own palette,
sense of self.
Work within it.
Make it yours so when
others see that combination
they think of you.
Your essence, your style.

Making a
living
is not
the same
thing as
making
a life

To write means to rewrite.
To paint means to work over your marks again.
To cook means to stir.
To sing means to rehearse.
To sew means to cut the edge.
To knit means to stitch one by one.

Life is half gift, half work.
You can enhance the first
by adding more of the second.

Such is life

Colours, like features, follow the changes of the emotions.

What fun Sir Isaac Newton must have had way back in 1666 discovering the interaction of colour. Clever him worked out that pure white light passed through a prism separates into all the visible colours. Does this sound just like the way you feel on a day when your emotions are fractured? You see, each colour is comprised of a single wavelength and cannot be separated any further into other colours. Our emotions are a bit like colour in the way they cannot be separated from our history and, just like our emotions, colour perceptions are subjective. Colour has a psychological effect on our mood. Colours also reflect our mood. We can also learn from colour.

1. Communicate.
Colour gives away the way we are feeling. It reflects our mood. Choose appropriate colours to communicate your feelings clearly. Knowing the effect of colour can make your home more meaningful, more inviting.

2. Same same, but different.
It was Newton who set out the colours of the spectrum in a circular diagram, the colour wheel painters still use. An identical shape expresses a different emotional mood with each colour variation.

3. A little competition is a good thing.
Competing colours are complementary. Complementary colours sit opposite each other on a colour wheel and when mixed in proper proportion make a neutral grey or black. Two complementary colours next to each other make the other appear brighter.

4. Harmony.
The comfortable feel in a room is due to colour harmony and juxtaposition.

5. It's what you believe.
The ancient Egyptian and Chinese practiced chromotherapy, sometimes called light therapy or colourology, which involved using colours to heal. It's still used today as a holistic or alternative treatment. Red to stimulate the body and mind and increase circulation. Yellow to stimulate the nerves and purify the body. Orange to heal the lungs and increase energy levels. Blue to soothe illnesses and treat pain. Indigo to alleviate skin problems.

6. Sensitive.
When describing our emotions we're sensitive to different nuances. Describing colour is the same, the words used to describe a tone have a different association for each of us. Both are open to interpretation.

We see and use colour constantly. To be aware it has different meanings in different cultures can add to the joy of it.

RED is evocative, more than any other colour it symbolises strength. In many creation myths the earth is red. It's the colour of life itself. In Hebrew tradition the first man was formed from red clay, while in Polynesia life began with a woman made from red sand. It's used ritualistically in ceremonies relating to creating and sustaining life, and death. The colour of fertility, red can create excitement, evoke urgency or cocoon you in a room. It attracts and repels, is the colour of love, lust, passion, romance, urgency and the blood which is intrinsic to life. Red evokes feelings from warmth and comfort to anger and hostility.

YELLOW has a place of honour, is attention seeking and good enough to eat. It makes you think of butter. Linked to the sun in most cultures, it is associated with happiness, evokes warmth and brilliance. It represents radiance and light. Bright, clear, and stimulating it's used to portray hopefulness, joy, and energy. Saffron robes make it the colour of Buddhism, while in ancient Greece and Rome the most beautiful saffron material was reserved for priests and muses. In China it symbolises the centre of the earth and is associated with rebirth.

BLUE was once a rare colour, is trustworthy and resonates with beauty, purity and wisdom. Some blue tones are used with specific meaning in Christian and Islamic religions. It projects an image of power, professionalism, and credibility. Blue can also be calming and give a feeling of tranquillity, along with sadness or indifference. It was only after the fifteenth century that the west depicted water in blue. Perhaps it's the world's most favourite colour because a clear blue sky means a sunny day.

PURPLE has been associated with spirituality, power, mysticism, and eroticism, since the dawn of time — worn by Roman senators, Indian maharajahs and modern European royalty. It is a healing colour related to mind, body and soul.

GREEN is nurturing and natural. It represents adventure and ecology. Green is associated with moisture and the earth and tells of the coming of spring and about fertility, the growth of food, and the continuance of life. When contrasted with black shadows it shows height, depth, density and a lushness of growth. In classical Arabic the words green, vegetation, grass and paradise are all derived from the same etymological root.

BLACK is emptiness, the lack of all colour, or an exhaustive combination of pigments. Our prehistoric ancestors used charcoal to express themselves, while black ink has been around since the Chinese used lampblack in the third millennium BC. Black is contradictory, simultaneously representing death and the womb of new beginnings. In the Middle Ages black represented ambivalent values until the fifteen century when, due to success with dyeing techniques, it was chic to be seen in black. During the Reformation sombre dress was a sign of humility and modesty. In the sixteenth century it became the colour of mourning. Never out of fashion, it is a symbol of elegance, a colour for all occasions.

WHITE is full of possibilities and luminosity. It represents purity, a silence emanates from it as it represents the warmth that allows things to blossom. The purest of whites have been used to honour gods and the dead. It comes in an endless variety, including clouds, a ray of light, shells, stars, milk and pearls. It's impossible to dye fabric white.

If you do not **ask** for what you want you may not get it.
It is very hard for people to second guess what it is you want.

AMARETTI DI SARONNO
SPECIALITÀ
MARCA DEPOSITATA
LAZZARONI
D. LAZZARONI & C.
SARONNO
Live your own life instinctively. One that feels like you.
Be authentic.
SOLA CHE DETIENE IL GENUINO PROCESSO
DI FABBRICAZIONE DEI VERI
AMARETTI DI SARONNO
PRINTED IN ITALY

Let's eat out

Waiter: Party of one?

One: Yes please (I enjoy my own company).

Waiter: Are you expecting anyone else?

One: No, I'm eating alone (I want some good food, don't feel like cooking tonight, and enjoy being out and about in stimulating surroundings).

Waiter: I have this table for you.

One: Please don't hide me in the corner (I want to be amongst other people. I'm not afraid or ashamed to be eating alone. I care enough about myself to take myself out).

Waiter: Would you like to eat at the bar? Or I have a table if you would prefer it.

One: Yes please, the bar (I won't feel self-conscious as there will be other ones also eating alone) Restaurants and cafes who care about those wanting to eat alone have alternative types of seating and wine by the glass. Stay loyal to them and take the trouble to get to know the staff. They will be happy and make you feel welcome anytime as they realise you've come for their food and not the company of others. Ones are amongst their most flattering customers. One easy way to spot a café or restaurants that understands ones is to see if they have magazines or books as company for those eating alone to get lost in. You'll find many ones eat breakfast or brunch out alone as it's a good way to treat yourself without feeling everyone around you is a romantic couple.

There are lots of stories of ones I could have included. Ones who made up the special mix at the places I have started. Without them it would have been impossible to achieve anything. They have a 'now, not when' attitude. I'm sure you know the kind, wonderful ones to be relied upon. Getting on with life, not dependent on a partner.

Now.
Not when.

Caroline was the first. She knew how to make a room glow. Amongst the housemaids at The Russell she shone straight away and was so good at her job she became the manager. She won my heart with the way she cared for everything she worked with, including the people. One was her sister, whom she bought to work with her. Add valuing family into her mix.

She joined in at The Bathers' Pavilion and shone there too. She had never worked a day in a restaurant so with this in common we shared a shoebox of an office. We chose and wrote the wine list together. Add a great palate into her mix. She left to study the science of making wine and, yes, was dux of her year. Years later she's winning trophies. No surprise. You just have to believe you can.

Smile mantras.

Mona Lisa just hangs about and smiles all day at people she doesn't know and never looks exhausted. Look where it's got her. Imagine if we all followed her example and smiled at ten people we don't know every day. We could give ourselves a point for each person. Double it when they smile back. Ten if they say something spontaneous and you engage. It doesn't matter if you don't get a response. You'll be exercising those cheek muscles of yours that communicate to the brain that you are happy.

What fun to be a smile researcher. They have identified many different types of smiles. A French physician, Guillaume, first recognized an anatomical distinction in the mid-nineteenth century when his research on the physiology of facial expressions identified two distinct types of smiles. A Duchenne smile involves contraction of both the zygomatic major muscle, which raises the corners of the mouth, and the orbicularis oculi muscle, which raises the cheeks and forms crow's feet around the eyes. A non-Duchenne smile involves only the zygomatic major muscle. Many of the lucky researchers have concluded the Duchenne smiles indicate genuine spontaneous emotions since most people cannot voluntarily contract the outer portion of the orbicularis oculi muscle.

Biologists think the smile originated as a sign of fear. They've traced it back over thirty million years to a 'fear grin' stemming from monkeys and apes who often used barely clenched teeth to tell predators they were harmless.

We have many different types of smiles. We all know some are sincere and others not. They communicate feelings of warmth towards another, love, happiness, pride, contempt and embarrassment. You can never wear a real one out.

A smile will let you in when a knock is never heard.

Like abandoned keys,
loose and sleeping in drawers,

once so important,
old address books can seem to be just
clutter, full of history
long past,
or viewed as opportunities to reconnect
with the inhabitants you
once had so much in
common with.

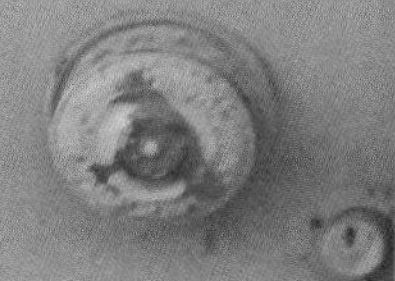

Silence cannot really be described.
It is not the absence of sound.
It makes it possible to notice sound.
It is still, but its stillness is constantly moving.
It is nothing, but a nothing filled with everything.

It is aware, but may move unaware.
It is love, but a love that lets hatred be.
It is wise, but its wisdom only fools can know.
It has a shape, the shape of the moment.
It has its own sound, but can only
be heard when the mind is still.
Unceasingly, it speaks the truth without
uttering a single word.

Dorothy S Hunt, *Only This!*

I'd learnt to put
myself second.
The past few years
have been about
learning who I am.
Not through someone else,
but through me.

After pain your heart expands
and grows back even bigger.
So it is with childbirth and renovations.

Love what others don't.

Call me mad, but I love to renovate. I adore giving old buildings new life. Just like your relatives, renovations seem to have an influence on who you become. They demand patience, decisions, and there is a need to consider others. As the aim is improvement, it doesn't matter where you start, you end up with something different from that with which you began. Somehow it always seems more grown up and prepared for the world. Houses standing side by side, all in a row, tell you who is the most developed, and it's not a matter of money.

The desire to renovate is a feeling thing. I get an 'I'm in trouble' feeling when I arrive at the threshold. It's been the patina, sometimes the light, always the potential. While renovations eat your money quite unlike anything else, they give it back tenfold when you open each drawer that holds food in a way that's easily accessed, see the hydrangeas through the bathroom window, or reach for that book from a shelf you pondered over. A passion for change and building can find it's way into your heart and sustain you through what others call 'b….y renovations'.

The love affair began with my first house. A small cottage, in a village suburb, exactly the same shape as the houses I drew when I was little. Front door in the middle of two windows and a large lemon tree out the back, while the front verandah and a frangipani gave it an Australian feel. I've watched the same two trees grow in my gardens since. They make it feel like home. I played endlessly with the five small rooms. With not much furniture to push about it was nothing for the dining room to become the room to sit, and vice versa, at a whim. My knees let me bend to paint the walls way back then as I expressed myself with a thick brush of colour.

Our next home began with holes in the floor, wonderful shafts of filtered light from the spaces in the red tiled roof and no kitchen. It had been a boarding house in a housing commission area. In such bad disrepair I used the tiny brick courtyard as the location for a television commercial to raise money for homeless people. I saw what I had dreamed of become reality. Something old and worn out came to life, and I became hooked watching its transformation in the assured hands of craftsmen. I was in awe of what they could achieve with an honest day's labour.

Our three children were born into this home. I tried my hardest to give them spaces of their own that felt like them. Rooms that were safe, never used for punishment, an expression of the individual I thought they would become. Each unique. They've gone on to express themselves in a similiar way. Loving the old and making it new. Thankfully, living with renovations for much of their early lives doesn't seem to have put them off.

I fell in love with another building in desperate need of care, just around the corner from home. It became a labour of love, a small hotel, The Russell. It too had previously been a rundown boarding house and during the early building stages I needed a disinfectant bath when I came home each night. It was as if I'd served my apprenticeship on our home renovations and was ready for this more demanding, larger restoration that was to have a commercial use.

I'd had no training or experience in hotels but this didn't stop my husband trusting my intuition and I enjoyed rising to the challenge. Each room was different. I used colour, pattern and texture to give them their own unique shape and feel. Putting it all together I'd think about the people who might be going to stay in the rooms — who were going to either make the hotel work or not. There was a need to connect with an audience and for that audience to want to tell someone else about their experience. Word of mouth is a valuable reward.

It seems more amazing to me today than it was at the time that, totally inexperienced, we ventured into something untested. The Russell was Sydney's first boutique hotel. Prior to The Russell I had only worked with an invisible audience. You never directly see the reaction to pages you have made in a magazine, or images you have contributed to on a screen. They're just out there in the ether somewhere. This was different, a way to connect directly with people and give them a unique Australian experience.

Without project management expertise it's no surprise the money ran out toward the crucial end stage, renovations take all you can give them. Looking for relief, my father was approached for a loan. He declined, saying there would be greater satisfaction knowing we had done it all on our own. He was right. The restorations provided a good education. A steep learning curve in teamwork, decision-making, debt repayment, choice, a search for a point of difference, and juggling work, home and mothering. My oldest daughter learnt to stand amongst the rubble, encouraged by all around her. The reward was seeing an elegant building enjoying another chance, and being used by like-minded people. I'm not alone in feeling some of my strongest travel memories are of places I've stayed. Special small hotels with staff willing to tell you all they know about their cities.

The Russell left me with the sense renovating is a bit like having an operation. One that fixes a bad back and makes you mobile again. Both take a team of specialists, consultation to arrive at logical solutions and good results. With building works you have your health, and all your faculties, at the time of getting your idea, you get the disease when you make your choice to take on the renovations, lose some freedom when you are tied down during the planning and building stage, which is similar to the convalescent stage. Recovery is complete when the last hammer disappears and the paintings are hung.

Moving from the inner city to an old house near the beach felt like heaven, despite the work ahead. More restorations to create a little more room, and a garden to plan and build. Again, this house was Australian in style, verandah all around. Its design, conceived eighty or so years earlier, was perfect. All it needed was love. Nuturing. An idyllic place to live, the water sparkled nearby, we had ducks, a chook that flew in and called it home, dogs, cats, a cubby house, and a lane full of people we loved sharing it with. I was as happy as a pig in mud working from home. There was balance in my mothering and work life, and I felt it possible to have it all.

Nurturing involves imagination. Restoration involves inventiveness and making a home requires spontaneity and a need to bypass what is now conventional, minimalism. I think spaces are at their best when they have a feeling of warmth that speaks of the people who inhabit them. Of their particular creativeness.

Sadly, after about fifteen years there my marriage was spent and I had to move. When the time came to part from this house I'd thought would be mine for life it was extremely hard. One of the hardest decisions I have had to make. It always is when parting with things you have created and love. They're never really yours, just yours for a while. Happily nobody can take your memories away, they belong just to you.

I had the chance to test my theory that buildings can find a new usefulness and give back in my next, largest, most exciting and exacting project to date, the restoration of the old Bathers' Pavilion on the beach at Balmoral.

Some of my earliest memories are of Balmoral as I spent much time on the beach as a child. I have fond memories of it not being crowded, the sand hot enough to make me jump, and my brothers sailing there. The Bathers' Pavilion housed the toilets we preferred not to use. It felt decrepit, and was. During my later teenage years my father would take us to dinner in the restaurant that occupied a small part of it, to give my mother, who had had a heart attack, a rest from cooking. I loved sharing the family news that dominated the conversation but it also gave me an appreciation of the beauty of eating out.

Years later I found myself dreaming about and planning for a new future for a wonderful old building that had always been in the background. I saw it becoming a small hotel with a café and restaurant downstairs, a place that locals would feel proud of, want to visit and share. Based on my travel experiences and those as a

diner, I went about creating what I would have wanted to find. Somewhere that showed the passion of those who owned it. A rarely frequented restaurant was already operating in about half of the ground floor. Tired and worn out, it was begging for a new life.

I began by pulling up the hideous dirty synthetic commercial carpet and polishing the concrete floor with the idea that people could walk in with sand between their toes. With no budget for new tablecloths, I ripped and sewed pieces of calico to cover worn tables. Boards were painted with green chalk paint, for the daily, handwritten menus, my misspelling corrected by staff. Perhaps this is a good place to confess my dyslexia. Just when I started to feel as though I was getting somewhere, a local popped in to tell me she knew the name of a good decorator. Restaurant lesson number one. You can't please everyone.

To make the inside feel harmonious I borrowed the colour palette from what was directly outside. I bought a bucket of sand in for the painter so he could match the colour of the walls to it. Picnic rugs and beach towels hung casually over hooks by the door. I collected early Australian pieces of furniture and brought things in from home, creating what people would eventually refer to as 'the Bathers' look'. It was a combination of textures, eclectic rustic pieces, a fusion of things from different places to enhance the eating experience. I especially love playing with the placement of things. It was nothing to re-hang pictures just before a service began and over the years I kept adding bits and pieces, small finds. They came to represent a giving back, a thank you to customers and regulars, who would nod knowingly when they saw the latest addition.

Starting out was tough. Wine distributors weren't prepared to sell wines being produced by the smaller, boutique wine makers unless I took their large producer mainstream offerings too. So I found myself enjoying dealing directly with owners of small vineyards and improving my wine knowledge and palate by doing so. When an insurance broker asked if there was a man he could speak to, I changed companies. Despite having been a credit card merchant at The Russell for years I was asked to provide all sorts of references. It was 1988 and it seemed hard to find anyone to believe in the project.

Running a restaurant, as those who have done it will know, is hard work with very little financial reward for the long hours and investment. Despite the challenges, it's worth it. Little can beat the look in someone's eye when they say 'Thank you, that was great. We'll be back.' Or observing customers who don't say it, but keep returning. They keep you going. Best of all pleasures is in seeing a customer arrive looking fraught and harassed and leaving relaxed and happy.

Within months of opening I lodged development plans with the local council, and later with the Heritage Council, to restore the dilapidated, leaky, old building. I wanted to give it a quintessentially Sydney feel. It involved a complete rebuild as the building had concrete cancer and had not been fully maintained for longer than anyone could remember. The plan was to use the remaining ground floor area as a café, and add bedrooms for a small boutique hotel, on the unused first floor. A small group of local residents didn't agree with my idea and staged a very vocal campaign against the proposal. During the years that followed, I tried my hardest to understand their point of view but found it difficult to reason. I was never able to think of another permissible use within the zoning possibilities that would have as little impact on traffic and noise, as the hotel guests would be sleeping when the residents were, to be able to fund the restoration and protect and guarantee the building's future while taking full advantage of the position and view.

When the plans were fresh and received publicity I would regularly get phone calls from people who were thinking about taking on similar building projects in public buildings. They would ask me how my plans were progressing. As time passed their calls stopped. I feel sure the publicity about the difficulties I was having killed any inspiration others may have had and they felt it all too hard to follow suit. Perhaps we should have formed a support group.

Despite attending too many council meetings to count — and always having the majority vote in favour of the plans — those determined to stop the hotel remained vigilant. The whole process took almost ten years. Fighting legal battles to renew the lease and renovate the building at my expense had an enormous cost. State and local government laws changed, there were four court cases and two separate Council Plans of Management. The approval was finally given without the hotel rooms, or what I now fondly think of as heartbreak hotel, and building work began. The restoration works took a year, during which time the restaurant was closed.

This long drawn-out process process taught me that some people are vehemently fearful of change. Wanting control over their situation means fear drives them to imagine an outcome that may not be reality, one they think will bring them discomfort. I learnt too that to have a cause in common is enough to add meaning to people's lives. Sometimes with little concern for how destructive it may be to others. A day or two after we reopened I spotted one protestor, wearing a suede jacket, camel pants and leather brogues, beginning a self tour through Bathers'. I asked if he would like me to show him around but he quickly retreated saying he wasn't properly dressed for the occasion. A short while later another protestor, also a driving force behind the campaign, told me she wished she'd accepted my invitation for a cup of tea and to be taken through the plans at the beginning of the process. She thought we had a lot in common after all. Certainly there would have been less traffic with a hotel.

Having ensured the building was preserved and seen Bathers' reopen successfully I knew the work of all involved had paid off. I stayed for a few years and loved seeing the building being enjoyed, still do. Not wanting to be in debt for the next ten or more years I parted ways, having made a dream a reality. I'm convinced dreaming of solutions for disused buildings is better than no dreams. The restaurant has given happy memories to the hundreds of people who have had many special experiences there over the last twenty-one years. I'm just one of many.

I've enjoyed making a new life, one that includes building blocks in painting and fine art, and after some renovations find myself living in a home that was once, many moons ago, a bakery. I like the fact that it seems to give others pleasure too. It feels like a snail's shell to me. I have played and nurtured. Every wall drilled in that 'there's nothing more empowering than a woman with a drill' kind of way. It's a living thing this house of mine. Those in partnerships take part of their homes with them each time they leave together. Perhaps a home is even more important to a one as it's just yours and only you become intimate with it.

It takes two to tango
but being happy with yourself
makes it easier
to be happy with somebody else.

Fall in love
with yourself.

'Two roads diverged in a wood,
and I took the one less travelled by.
And that has made
all the difference.'

Robert Frost

Treating people like you want to be treated is a good rule for life.

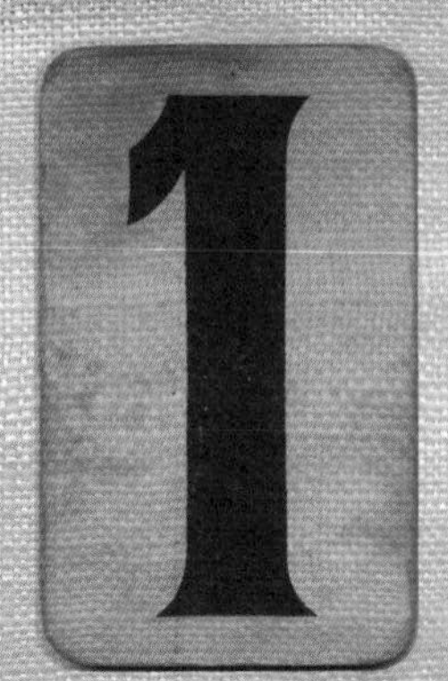

I remember reading a newspaper article years ago about **Pierre Omidyar** and the surprisingly personal approach he had taken when eBay had a technical glitch. It was in 1998, at the time when the company he founded went public. They had more than a million registered users and were suffering growing pains when one service interruption lasted for twenty-two hours. Omidyar directed his staff to make 10,000 phone calls to the site's top users to apologise and assure them everything possible would be done to keep the site up and running in the future.

Omidyar believes people are basically good and that if you give them the benefit of the doubt you're rarely disappointed. This belief, his fascination with computers since high school, determination, and a simple idea, turned eBay into a huge success.

The idea for online auctions came about over a dinner when his girlfriend (now wife), Pam, said she couldn't find anywhere to trade the Pez containers she had been collecting. These colourful little plastic sweet dispensers were for years modelled on classic cartoon characters. Omidyar was intrigued and worked through technical problems to establish a direct person-to-person online auction of collectible items. He began by creating Auction Web, a simple prototype on his personal web page. It took off. People registered and traded an unimaginable variety and number of things. The small fee he collected from each sale financed the expansion of the site. Business grew through word of mouth, and Auction Web added a Feedback Forum, allowing buyers and sellers to rate each other for honesty and reliability. By mid 1997, the year the company changed its name, it was hosting nearly 800,000 auctions a day. eBay's prospering. There are about ninety-five million users, selling in around 45,000 categories. It's expanding into Europe and Asia, especially China and India.

The Omidyars plan to give away all but one percent of their fortune over the next twenty years and have created Omidyar Network to help empower people in developing countries to lift themselves out of poverty. More than two billion people worldwide live on less than US$2 a day, and another estimated two billion struggle with problems of inadequate housing or lack the financial resources and stability to procure basic services, and protect themselves from economic shocks. These four billion people represent a socio-economic class referred to as the base of the pyramid. So there are two good reasons Pierre Omidyar is a favourite one.

Close both eyes to see with the other eye.

Rumi

When I was about eight,
almost old enough to know better,
I ran away from the dentist's chair.
My mother retrieved me from the street.

I should have learnt the lesson then:

Face your fears

or they will come back to bite you.

We all need some help sometimes

How many times have you seen

Look Good Feel Great

written on a magazine cover?

Shouldn't it read ...

Feel Good Look Great

Talking and Listening

Talking is a matter of habit.
Listening too.
Unless we listen to what we say
we say things we don't really mean.
Or that are misunderstood.
Do you listen to what you say?
To yourself?

1

'I take the opportunity each day offers'.

We all leave a trace. If we touch others it's a successful one. **Andy Goldsworthy** touched my life with his transient sculptures while I was at art school. It's difficult to know where his work starts and nature begins. He creates a new perception and understanding of the land by working instinctively with nature. The processes of life within and around an endless range of things: snow, ice, leaves, bark, rock, clay, stones, petals, feathers, and twigs, interests him. These processes continue as he leaves his work sitting in nature. Decay is implicit. His natural materials are in sympathy with nature's cycles and he's undeterred by changes in the weather, which may melt or wash away a structure. His materials aren't independent of their surroundings; they sit within them and tell how they came to be. Looking, touching, place, form and material are all inseparable from the final work. Place is found by walking, direction determined by weather and season. If it's snowing, he works in snow, in autumn it will be leaves; a blown over tree becomes the source for twigs and branches. Movement, change, light, growth and decay are nature's lifeblood, and the energies that run through his work. Nature is continually in a state of change and that change is the key to understanding. As, or before they disappear, he photographs them. Simply. No tricks. Born in a house edging a green belt, Andy Goldsworthy worked on farms as a labourer from the age of thirteen. He feels repetitive farm tasks are similar to the routine of making sculpture. 'A lot of my work is like picking potatoes: you have to get into the rhythm of it'. Andy believes one of the beauties of making art is that an artist is able to use all they've learned from life to inform their work. A process he hopes continues until the end. Reason enough to be a favourite one.

‘We meet naturally on the
basis of our sameness
and grow on the
basis of our differentness.’

Virginia Satir

'Don't cry for a man
who has left you.
The next one may
fall for your smile.'

Anon

Above all have a good time

1

Julia Child's *Mastering the Art of French Cookery, Volume One* in paperback, was my first cookbook. My mother used it and gave me a copy when I got married. I used to take it to bed to read. First published in 1961, Julia gives clear and detailed instructions to lead you through her recipes. It made me want know more about food. Although she wrote her original books with others I've always felt it was Julia who gave me the confidence to always have a good time while cooking because she preached being relaxed, enjoyment over perfection and that once the basics were mastered it was simply a matter of enjoying yourself by cooking with love. Born in 1912, Julia was a towering 188 cm tall. Her career included advertising, volunteering as a research assistant for a US government intelligence agency in Ceylon (now Sri Lanka) and China. She served with the Office of Strategic Services during World War II, the huge spy network created by President Franklin Roosevelt and forerunner of today's CIA. She was a one for thirty-four years, didn't cook before marrying, and made her television debut at fifty using humour while cooking an omelette for the promotion of her first book. The producers wanted more and so began 'The French Chef', which became the longest-running program in the history of American public television. She started a cooking school and wrote eighteen books. She insisted mistakes were not the end of the world, just part of the game, which is more than enough to make her a favourite one. Her early experiments became her core belief: cooking was an art to be studied. True to herself, genuine and unpretentious, she was an advocate for the good life and the joys of the table.

Don't
label
others
if
you
do
not
want
to
be
labelled
yourself.

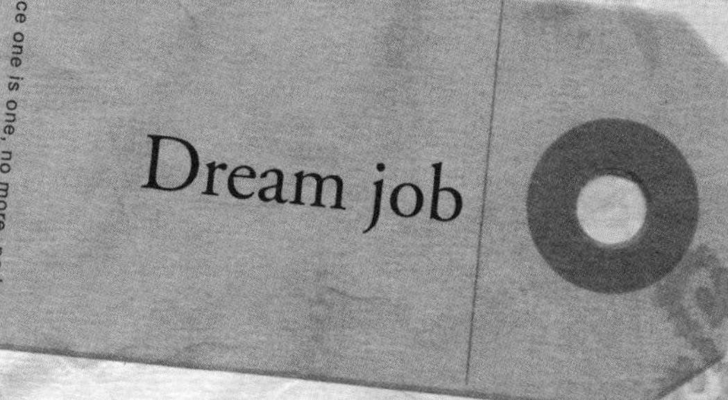

Dream job

I want my next job to be the person who gives lipstick their names.

I imagine it to be in Paris. I will be able to tell jokes in French, live on the Ile St Louis, bicycle to work, and enjoy the long summer twilights. Having not worn lipstick until recently I am fascinated by the appropriateness of their names:

Lover • Subtle • Passion • Surprise • Desirable • Imagination

As they just seem to get it right I wonder if it's a committee decision?

Or is it someone, like me, just bringing a little colour into our lives?

I choose them for their colour, which is affected by my mood, so what bemuses me is that I forget their names until I have put one on. Only then do I remember they've the uncanny knack of rising to the occasion. Their names seem appropriate for the outing we are about to embark on. For the first meeting with the publisher of this book I subconsciously chose Imagination. Perhaps my next colour will be called Freedom.

We all need a little space sometimes

Resilience

We all know hard people. They're tough.

It's a quality I don't admire. In fact it's one I run from. I've learnt tough people create barriers that make it impossible to become close to them. It's usually out of self interest. They don't seem able to consider another point of view.

Resilience is different. It's a quiet inner strength. An attitude. One that allows you to feel and be compassionate while sticking up for yourself. To spring back without feeling bitter. It's a skill worth cultivating.

If you are apprehensive and feel beaten you will be. Remaining positive is what it's all about. There's always some, one thing to cling to that's good about any situation. Resilience means looking for this positive twist when there's not an obvious one. It means not taking things personally; thinking like a survivor and not a victim. A sense of humour helps too. Asking if … or when … doesn't. It'll defer your happiness and is a sure recipe for disappointment.

Our talent and skills are different from our inner strength. The first two we rely on constantly, while our inner muscles are used mostly when tested. Acting with resilience means being true to your self, aware of the ethical dimensions of your decisions, using what you've learned from the past, and taking the trouble to imagine the likely consequences of your actions before you act. We all admire firm, resilient individuals. True ones.

Be kind to yourself.
Do something 'just for you' each day.

It is important to take time out.
To recharge.
Nurture yourself.

Then reconnect.

‘I know what it’s like to be married and I know what I’m missing out on, but I also know what it is to be single and the freedom that it brings.’

‘I was on my own for a long time. I have had several relationships and now I am married. I could not have the relationship I now have without the time I had on my own.’

To experience both
surely makes you richer.

We express ourselves in the way we dress. Who we are. What we believe in. It's an act of freedom and independence. It is a sign of our identity, culture, and self-respect.

The clothes we wear can simply be a means of protecting our bodies. To preserve some decency. Clothing, like language, also carries significant messages that shouldn't be underestimated. Our self image, self esteem, self confidence, and cultural identity are all projected in the clothes we wear. Those fortunate enough to have a real choice in what they wear use their clothes to send a message to those who care to observe them. The observer makes a judgement based on what an individual is wearing.

Someone in uniform is easily recognisable. Fashion victims too. Slavishly following trends makes you one of the pack. Using the same time and energy to express yourself and your emotions makes you a precious individual. Forget what someone else thinks is right. Follow your heart. Place emphasis on comfort and consider 'vintage'. It makes sense as it recycles, values and gives a new use to things. It honours history.

Linda Grant, in her book *The Thoughtful Dresser*, doesn't believe those who state they are not interested in clothes or what they wear. She says not caring about the way we look is usually a sign of depression, madness or resignation to our imminent death. Now that's enough to make you want to make an effort.

Please be sensitive about
'and partner'.
Not everyone has one.

Heartsease

Violets are a clever little perennial also known as Heartsease and Johnny-Jump-Up. In Shakespeare's *A Midsummer Night's Dream* when Queen Titania used it in her potion to make Bottom fall in love with her, it also had another name, Love-In-Idleness. They have heart-shaped leaves and were used by medieval herbalists when treating heart disease. Violets look best in the company of others. Gathering a posy feels like the soft heart of spring and teaches us to surround ourselves with like-minded people. With a prolific self-seeding habit of popping up all over the garden they give us another lesson. Encouragement not to be a shrinking violet.

All you have to do…

Asked of a preschool teacher:
‘Do you have children?’
Teacher:
‘No, I don’t.’
Advice from the four year old:
‘Oh, then here’s what you do.
You get an egg.
Look at men in the street and choose one.
A Dad will walk past you and if you like him,
and he likes you, you marry him.
He asks you or maybe you ask him.
Make sure you like him.
We will be your bridesmaids.’
There are fifteen or so girls in the class.

True story.

1 + 1

There's luxury in one on one.
To be with another one.
Just one.

The smallest thing makes a difference

once one is one, no more, no less.

Bag lady

I have these magic little silk bags that add a frisson to shopping. Lustrous and full of promise they fold up into nothing so I take them everywhere with me. Their joyous clear bright colours put a smile on the checkout chick's face every time. I've never had anything quite like them.

They're conversation starters given to me by a French friend who chose Schiaparelli hot pink and English postbox red. They are also a curious luxury as together they make me feel liberated and alive. The moment I get them out to fill with goodies I smile, and usually receive one from an onlooker. They're one of life's little pleasures.

At my store that has everything, run by a local family, they ask 'Got your bags?' Just as they do at the farmers market too. I like to think they appreciate them. Not because of their colour, but because those same old plastic bags (sure they're recyclable) don't do their work justice. The fresh produce they present has such wealth to it.

After the first few uses I felt a need to spread the word — if everyone had one the world would be a better place. My book club were given them as library bags. My

sister for document storage. My godson for toys. The possibilities seemed endless. I carried a spare with me at all times so someone who admired mine could have one. I felt capable of ridding the world of the sameness of green and plastic bags. I wanted the idea to catch on.

I became so keen on them I ordered a hundred for a charity fund raising event I was involved with. I learned the person who started the company (www.ecosilkbags.com.au) was a single mother working from home. She made them to earn a living while her children were at school. I was pleased to hear her idea had begun to catch on and sales were improving, despite the fact she had little time for marketing. She was just beginning to get them made in China. In a sustainable way she assured me.

Like everything, of course there are alternatives. If everyone had them they would become a uniform and perhaps the smiles they are capable of producing would diminish. Alternatives matter.

We all have the write of reply.

There's a difference between

reacting and responding.

You can't control other people,

but you can control

your response to them.

Think about it.

You may just change the way

you think or at the very least

the way you put it.

Don't hold a grudge.

Mandela, The Dalai Lama and Barack Obama all have reason to.

Instead they do good.

They empowered themselves.

Take their lead.

Find inspiration in your own life.

Rise to the challenges.

Make something from what you think you are missing out on.

The man who underestimates himself is perpetually being surprised by success, whereas the man who overestimates himself is just as often surprised by failure.

Bertrand Russell

We are what we think. Most people don't consider themselves rich. But have good health. And are probably good-natured. Some have passions they want to follow that make a quiet life seem dull. But for most people contentment is an achievement rather than a gift at birth. Achieving it involves both inward and outward effort. It depends partly on your circumstances, partly upon yourself. Those who live objectively, are affectionate and have a variety of interests tend to be fulfilled.

Marriage or a partnership is not an automatic source of bliss. It takes work and often ends in divorce. Some stick with it; too frightened of what life may be like without a partner. It can be too good to leave and too bad to stay. Our emotions are the slaves to our thoughts, and we are the slaves to our emotions.

A fresh start can be nerveracking. And exciting. Full of hope. Potential. Those first moments of independence. New beginnings feel crucial to success. We want to make connections, both intellectual and emotional.

The embarrassment of a first date, and the hope of subsequent ones that may or may not follow, make anyone feel like a teenager. Especially if you haven't dated for years. You want to look and feel your best. Give it your best shot. It feels like an audition and you have to decide which role you want. You'll feel cross-examined by family and friends. Especially your children if you have them. They will want to know 'Where did you… ?', 'How did you ...?' and 'Will you be …?'. You will tell them, politely of course, while feeling churned up inside because you have no idea if you should call, wait for him to call or simply forget the whole damn thing. You didn't like his blue suede shoes anyway.

You know the rules have changed. Or are there any? It's a brave new world you want to enter. How to begin is a big question. Trust the universe? Fate? An introduction from a friend? You're not desperate; just would like company, someone to share spontaneous things with. You've heard and read about successes using dating sites and know about the balance of life. That sometimes there are more single men than women. Or vice versa. It's not to do with a desire for celibacy, just a hazard determined by statistics. Each place needs a certain number of widows, bachelors and spinsters. Something that's accepted beautifully by the Italians.

We are different, we men and women. Remember Dr John Gray, of *Men are from Mars, Women are from Venus* fame who made much of it? He believes 'men are like emotional camels'. Camels walk through the desert for days without the need of any water. He believes the same applies to men. That they can spend days without the need for a feminine presence. Perhaps it's because

men, just like women, are sensitive to rejection and get nervous.

Just thinking about calling 'the one from last night' is the same for both sexes. The more we care the more pressure we feel. It's the thought of rejection. 'The one' may not feel the same.

All of us would prefer to avoid rejection. Being attracted to someone who's just not ready or wanting to be involved can be tricky. They may not necessarily want to share that kind of information. It might be they are involved with someone else. They just haven't told you about. It has nothing to do with you. It is about their current situation. There are many reasons many a call has not been made. Disappointing, but true.

In *What Men Want*, written by the committee of Gerstman, Pizzo and Seldes, they say sometimes just the thought of leaving a message and 'the one' not returning the call can be a major rejection for a man. It can also be the reason a man doesn't call in the first place.

It's all very complex or simple if you are given the chance to understand. Which means communicating openly from the start. Being honest and real. If the other party doesn't want to be then forget it. Avoid future disappointment.

Say what you mean.
Mean what you say.

Researching possibilities for gardening and building I came across Spanish Catalan architect **Antoni Gaudí** who stands out as an original, eclectic architect. One who formulated his own language, whose structures reflect natural forms. He is a favourite one for breaking with tradition. He was part of the Modernist movement, and incorporated mosaics in his flamboyant works to ensure no two corners of his buildings were the same. So it's no surprise both his parents were artists. As a child Gaudí suffered from rheumatic fever and spent a lot of time in isolation,

alone with nature.

It later became his inspiration. His first commission was for lamp posts and he designed menus for the cafe where Picasso's early work was shown.

Now, more than 150 years after his birth, his understanding of structure, colourful decoration, light and sculpture is testament to his ability to isolate himself from everything that could have disturbed his work. He put architectural procedures to the test and transformed his workshops into laboratories where he worked on experimental models.

Designing without artistic prejudice, he relied on experience, had a propensity for the tried and tested when it came to building methods, worked on saving energy and resources, and appreciated the common sense of practical rural people dedicated to work. Many of the twenty or so projects with exceptional personality that he directed, mostly in Barcelona, have gone from private to public ownership and in amongst them is Parc Güell, a peaceful garden with architectural elements in the Gràcia. It sits on a rocky hill called Montaña Pelada, or Bare Mountain, and was built between 1900 and 1914. Originally a housing development with views it is protected and isolated by a meandering surrounding wall made of rubble with inlaid ceramics. Originally divided into sixty triangular parcels, only three sold due to the outbreak of World War I. Gaudi's vision, based on playful intuition, was converted into a public park in 1922 and is now part of a UNESCO World Heritage Site. When signing his Architecture degree the scholar was unsure if he was a nut or a genius and believed time would tell. It has. Not accepted by his contemporaries and understood by few during his lifetime, I like to think that interest in his work now is due to an appreciation of his distinct individuality.

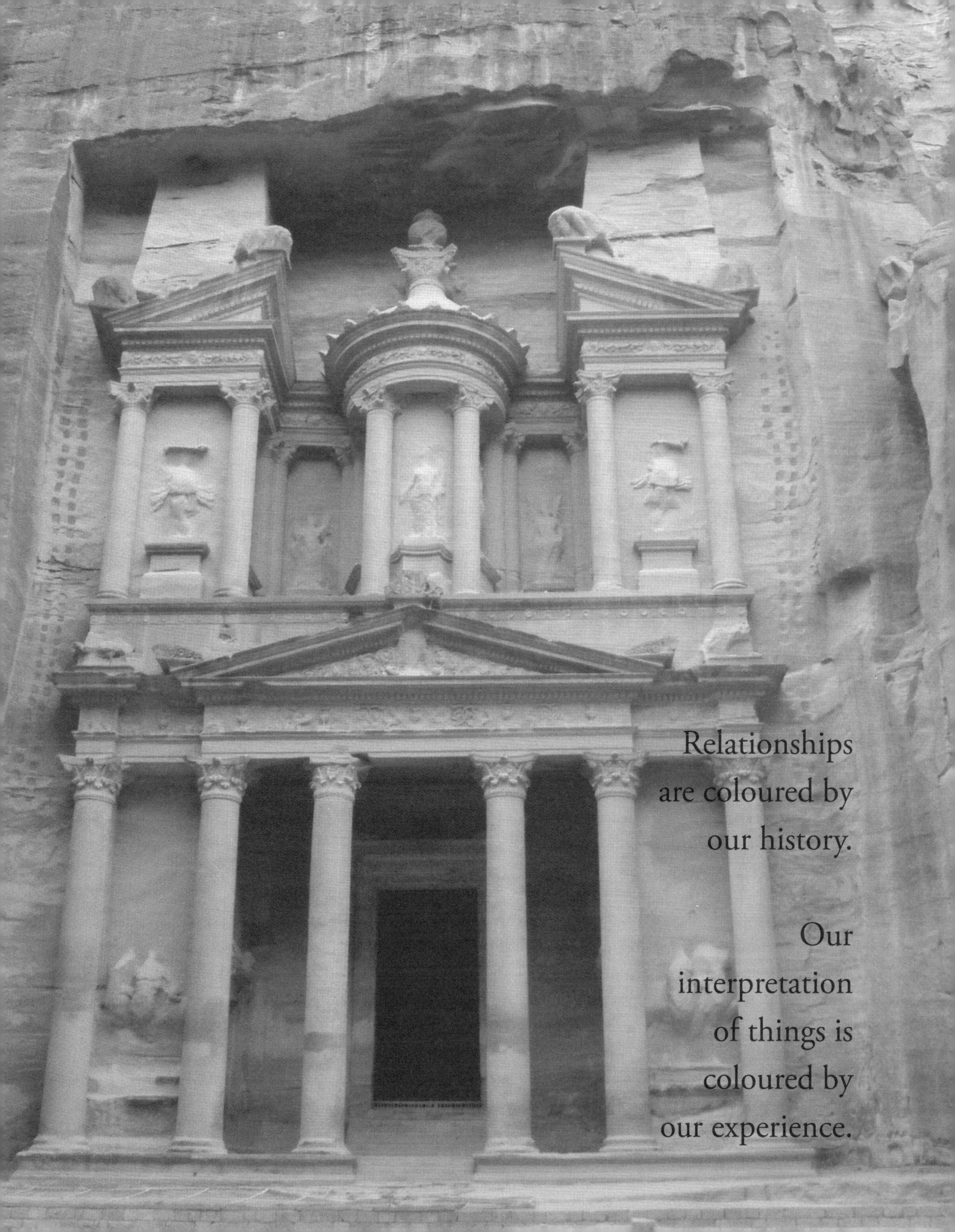
Relationships
are coloured by
our history.
Our
interpretation
of things is
coloured by
our experience.

J. D. SALINGER

Memories.

I don't think a house becomes a home until it holds some memories. I know mine didn't. Thoughts of people and things learnt from time spent in their company, usually around food, make me feel I can call it home. I love everything about it. It's far from immaculate. I believe there's no point in being a slave to housekeeping. I'd rather leave the bed unmade if it means seeing a friend, being late, or creative instead. The bed can wait while that moment of creativity I've have been waiting for just may not.

An old table sits smack bang in the middle of my home, once a bakery. It's in my kitchen. Nearby, a fireplace provides warmth in winter while the northern light shines through the window panes making patterns on the wooden surface. At times there are many around it, and sometimes just me as I sit with the newspaper spread between a bowl of flowers or fruit and a beloved cup of tea while the kitchen feels as calm as an empty church. The mail also seems to find its way there. The table holds many memories. Of projects made, of watching my son draw happily, birthday celebrations and what my children call interest tables. After a trip I set it with treasures from where I've just been. Sometimes I arrive home and know someone else has been. A newspaper spread across it tells me so. It also shares what they were thinking about while here. I may be alone but feel them with me.

The table I'm writing at now sits directly above it, sharing the same light, reminding me that food, family and friends are at the centre of my existence. Like light there's no permanence to their visits but memories of times shared linger and make up my life's patchwork. One I feel richer for.

I remember my brother and I playing underneath my parent's dining table — a sheet draped over it making us a home with white curtains. With the help of my dolls we instantly became mothers and fathers, made furniture from wooden blocks and cooked on an imaginary stove. It felt heavenly and was the centre of family life.

Special also is a heavy red saucepan, with a lid. It's oval and delicious things happen in it. It was my mother's and came to me via an extended holiday with my father after my mother died. It holds so many memories it makes me almost want to sing every time I use it. The warmth of my mother floods back to me. I see her nurturing in the kitchen and I hope my children will feel the same each time I slow-cook something for them in it, stir a soup or risotto. All they know for now is that 'it was my mother's'. One day it will have been 'my grandmother's and my mother's' as their memories attach themselves to that wonderful cadmium red pot that sits on top of the stove at all times.

What about you?

What homey childhood memories do you remember? What lessons can you take from them? The smell of onions becoming transparent in a pan, beeswax polish, a wet dog, a fence brimming with sweet peas or roses, crisp sheets dried with sunlight, a vegie patch waiting to be picked, shoes strewn across floorboards or a rug whose intricate pattern you tried to decipher?

Homes are like talking. Memorable when animated. Like art they depend on lucid expression and independent thought. They allow us to have an unspoken, ongoing conversation. They never know too much about anything and teach you about things you thought you already knew.

Our homes and our everyday things say a lot about us. They're valuable aspects of life. Our world. Walking through doors into inviting rooms that have a vividness and personality all their own is like poetry for the soul. There are all too few of them.

The Unknown

Leaving the familiar can be scary.
To know the value in something different
we first need to try it.
This involves risk.
We may move outside our comfort zone.
Become anxious even.
Or not.

It's a choice.
Your choice.

Change comes about by being emotionally honest.
About your feelings.
Own them, don't attribute them to someone else.
Make them count.
Show what you intend on the inside on the outside.

I
think
answers
are
much
more
beautiful
when
they

come out of questions.

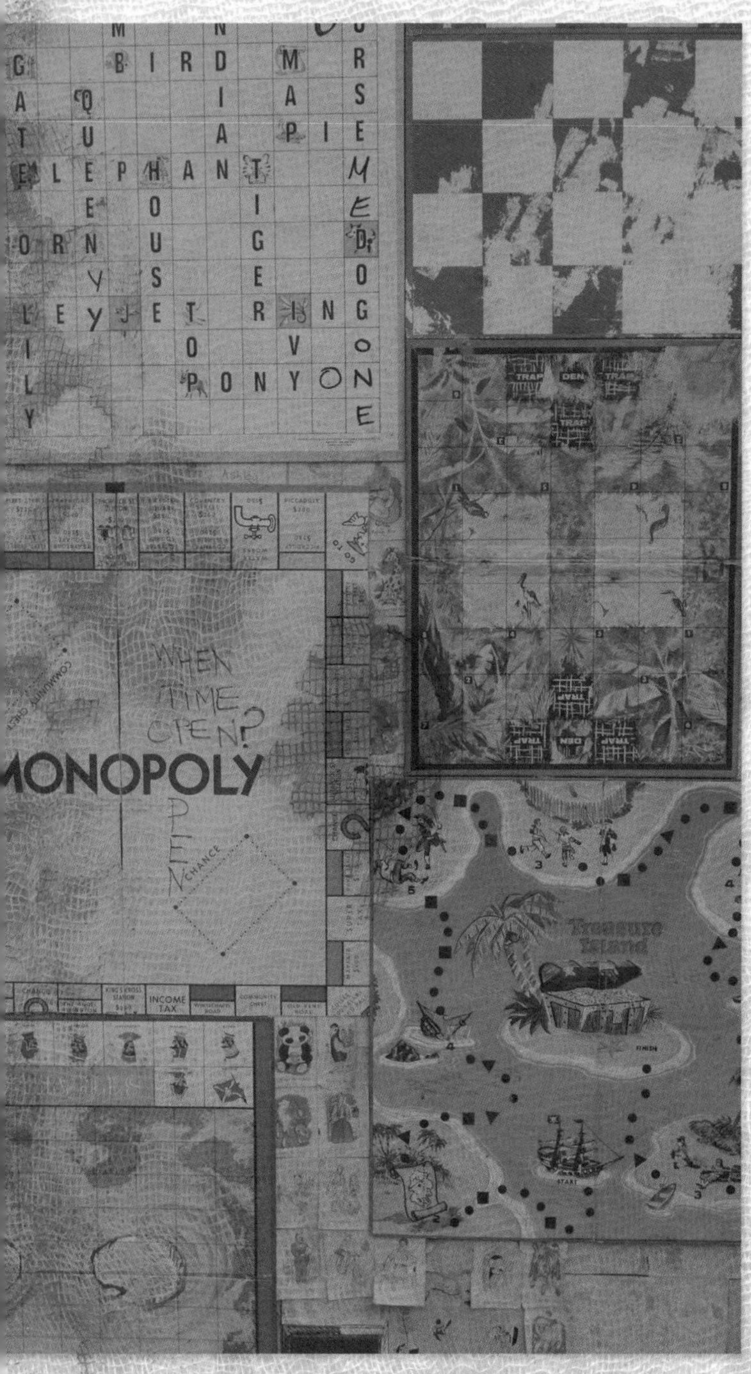

‘We should be mucking about all the time, because mucking about is enjoying life for its own sake, now, and not in preparation for an imaginary future. It’s obvious that the mirth-filled man, the cheerful soul, the childish adult is the one who has least to fear from life.’

Tom Hodgkinson,
The Freedom Manifesto

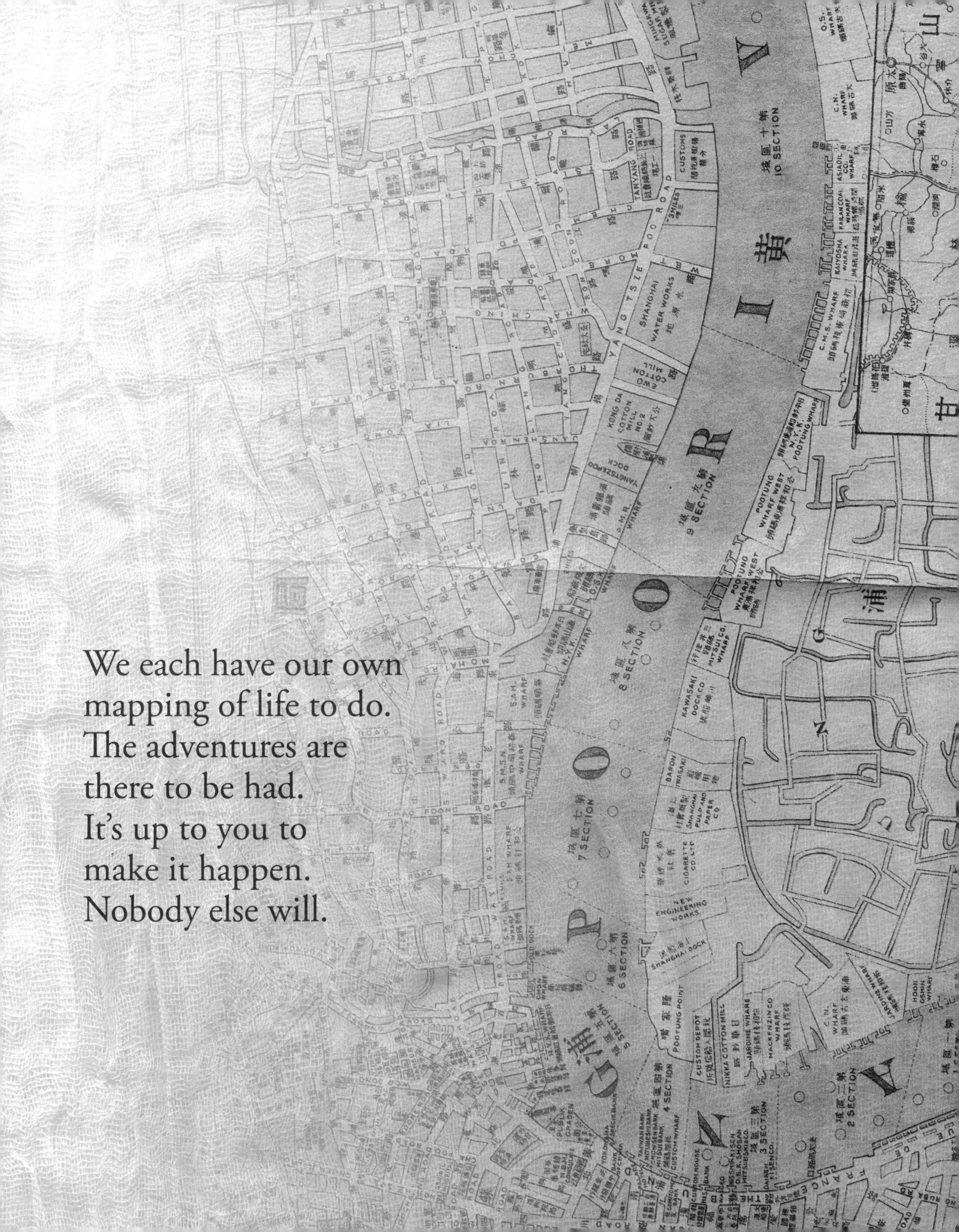

We each have our own
mapping of life to do.
The adventures are
there to be had.
It's up to you to
make it happen.
Nobody else will.

Life has its ups and downs.

But it's mostly about the in between.

I think I first heard about **Freya Stark** from my great aunt. Freya, the quintessential explorer, explored the Middle East, wrote two dozen books about her travels, and was a cartographer. Her English parents, who were keen travellers, were studying art in Paris when she was born in 1893. Much of her childhood was spent in northern Italy, she read a lot and for her ninth birthday was given *One Thousand and One Nights*, which lead to her fascination with the Orient. She learned French, and taught herself Latin. Freya studied history in London and during World War I worked as a nurse in Italy. In 1927 she discovered a passion for Arabic and Persian languages and traveled to Lebanon and Syria to study there. It was here she decided to make travel an end in itself.

Freya was one of the first Western women to travel through the Arabian deserts, often alone and with little or no baggage, into areas where few Europeans had been. She had extraordinary stamina, was witty and stubborn, overcame dysentery and malaria, and had a preference for bold dresses by French designers or personal versions of Oriental dress. By 1931 she had completed three dangerous treks into the wilderness of western Iran, in parts no Westerner had ever been before, and had located the long-fabled Valleys of the Assassins. During the 1930s she penetrated the hinterland of southern Arabia.

During World War II her knowledge of the Arab world and her determination were useful to the British secret services. Her eccentric, harmless, friendly demeanor was valuable in her dealings with political leaders in Egypt, Iraq, Syria, and Palestine. She contributed to the creation of a network aimed at persuading Arabs to support the Allies or at least remain neutral. She claimed her best achievement was the founding and running of the Brothers and Sisters of Freedom, a more or less secret organisation that supported the British Crown. Its members were English, Egyptian, Iraqi, and Indian. She died in her hundredth year. She's a favourite one for her courage.

1

'There can be no happiness if the things we believe in are different from the things we do.'

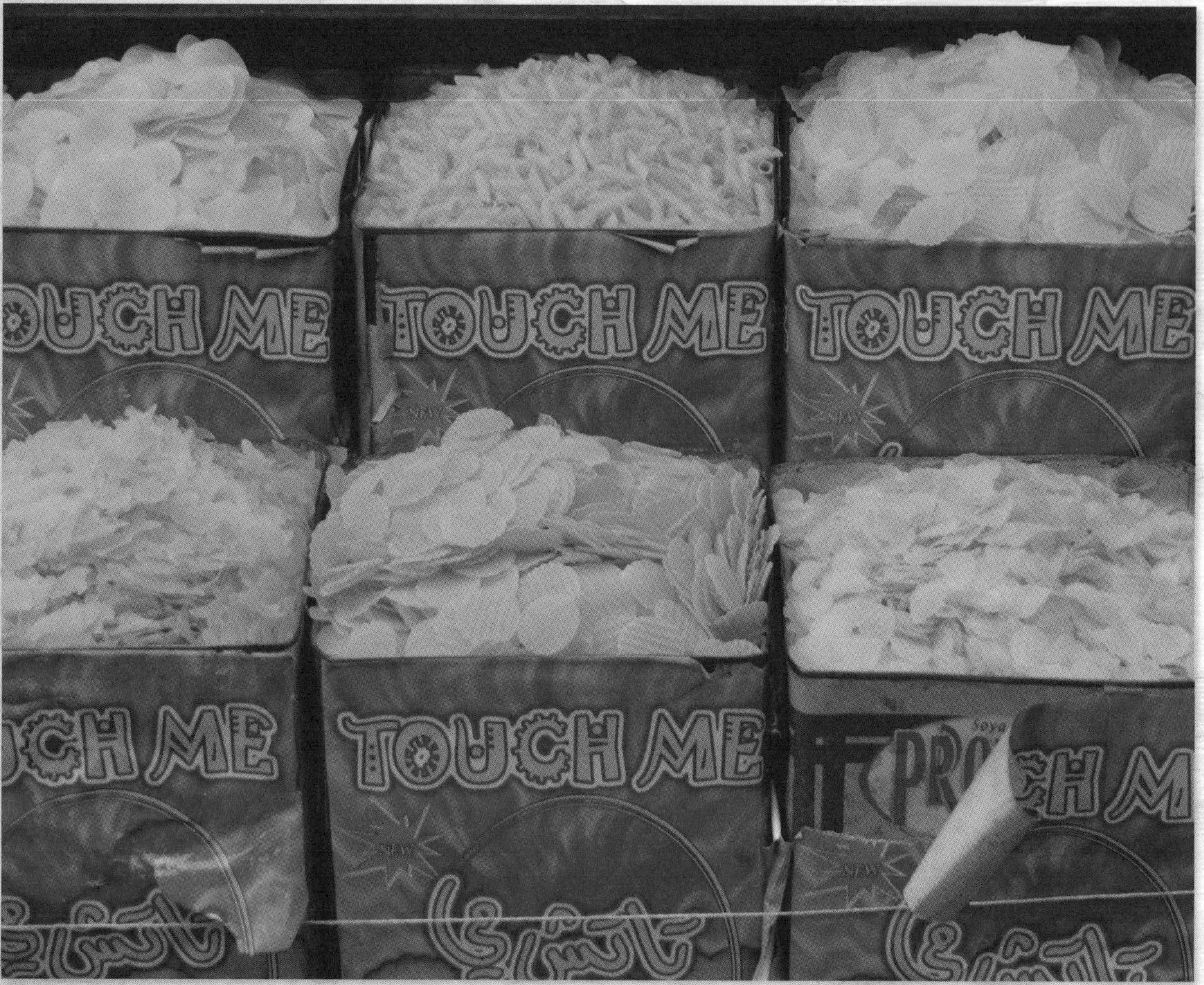
TOUCH ME
TOUCH ME
TOUCH ME
NEW

TAXI
٨٢٣٨

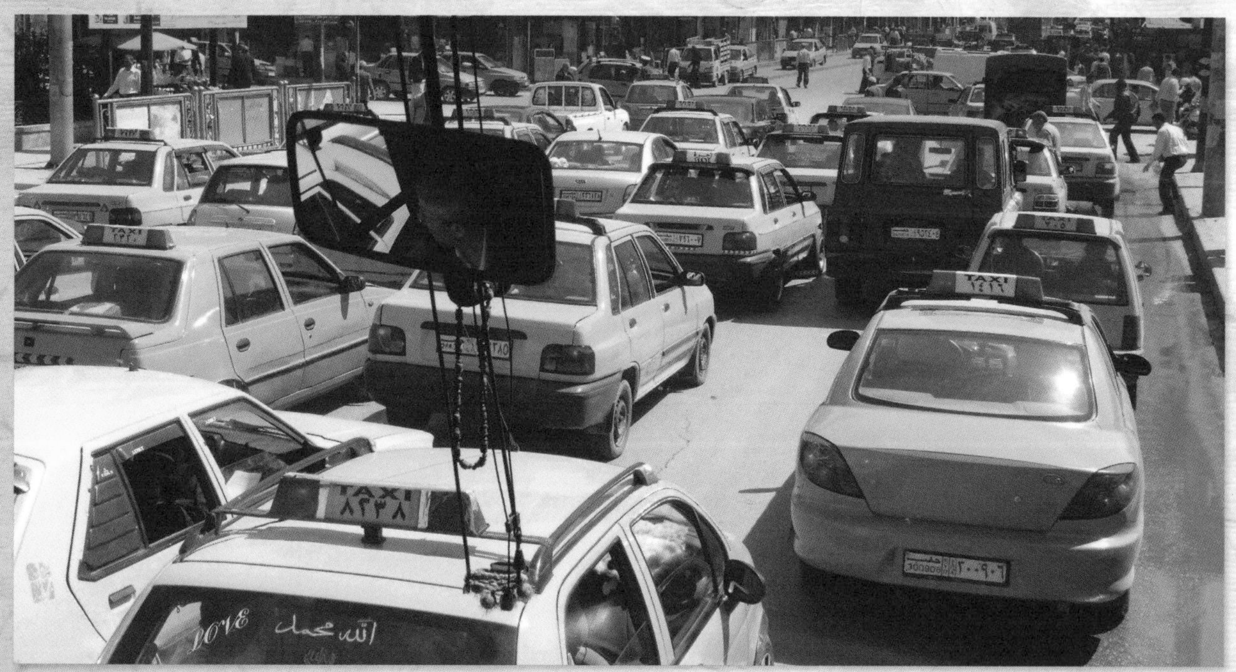

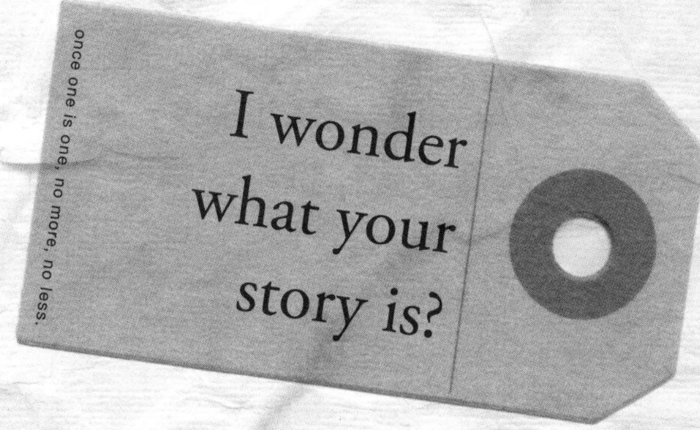

Are you like me, do you wonder where everyone is going? When I'm out and about I'm amazed at the number of people also going somewhere. Why shouldn't they be you ask. But where are they going? It's fascinating to imagine their lives while waiting at a set of traffic lights, or on the ferry, or in a cafe. I love to play a game — What's your story?

I imagine what they do, where they're going, and whom they may be meeting. Many people walk determinedly on their own; lots of cars have just one person. At airports the weary appear to be going home after business trips. Their relief is visible at the baggage point. I imagine they are thinking 'there's no place like home'.

The need for space and the way we regard each other varies with different cultures. The river of motorbikes that continually come straight at you as you cross a busy street in Hanoi is tenacious, so too is their unwritten law and regard for life so that they avoid you, just in time. The rhythm of cars around the Arc de Triomphe or any busy Italian road is mild in comparison. Yet they have one thing in common, you get a strong sense of the faces that come way too close for comfort, a rare smile, some clue about who they are and then they disappear just as quickly again out of your life.

It's a bit like when you go to the movies. You don't really make contact with anyone there either. Insulated from each other by the dark, the hush, and yet everyone shares the same story. That's about as far as it goes in social interaction.

There are few clues in the street or a crowded movie house that we all have one thing in common. We need friendship to sustain and support us. Like the ebb and flow of life, it can be enough just knowing someone 'is there' for you.

When times are tough we call on our friends. Support from friends can mean the difference between feeling you are facing something alone and feeling you have been heard, are empowered and prepared for whatever may arise next. It's a powerful tonic. I hope those I watch going to and fro are as lucky in their friendships.

Each of us.

Each of us is several, is many. Is a profusion of selves.
So that the self who disdains his surroundings is not the same
as the self who suffers and takes joy in them.
In the vast colony of our being there are many species
of people who think and feel in different ways.

Fernando Pessoa

When visiting another country be sure to talk to locals, ask them what they like and do, before you visit any museum or library, any site or famous town. Ask them to talk to you about their country, to tell you the names of things and how, traditionally, they have been made or fit together within their community. Walk with them through their bazaars and markets, ask for their stories, the voice of memory over their land. Taste their food, see where it is grown, leave the cities. Ask what they imagine is possible, about the changes they've felt, the spirituality and passions that bind them, the lessons time has taught. Take your time and do all you can to make sense of a real place, to know that you are not inhabiting an idea.

1
8
15
22
29

DETAILS

It's important to feel as
much at home in the world
as we do in our own surroundings

Dear one,

Now that you find yourself beginning a life on your own I thought it might be useful to share some everyday things I've learnt by making mistakes.

1. **Keeping it clean: laundry stuff.**
   Check labels. Choose the right temperature for your load.
   Don't mix colours … don't even think about it. The temptation is not worth it. You may cry over the result.
   Make separate coloured loads — red, blue, dark.
   Keep all your whites as a separate load.
   Lay woollens flat to dry. Never ever put them in the dryer. If you do, cut them up and patchwork a felted rug.

2. **Eat well: shop often.**
   Buy fresh, seasonal, organic produce and make it the best you can afford.
   Don't let price be your indicator. Make it flavour.
   Buy only what you need. Avoid offers of 'two for less', you'll rarely use the extra.

4. **Very versatile: Tomatoes.**
   Don't refrigerate those beautiful red balls of flavour. Leave them out in a bowl. Not just for their colour, for their taste. They don't like being cold.

5. **A quick meal: Steak.**
   Turn it once only. Leave it to rest.

6. **Roll your own: Pastry.**
   Use iced water from the fridge.
   Don't overwork the mixture.

7. **Cleaning up: In the shower.**
   While waiting for the water to heat up fill a bucket with the cold water. Use it on your plants.

8. **Do as I say, not as I do: Paperwork.**
   Pay your bills as they come in. They mount up.

Enjoy yourself.
The Goddess of Plenty.

There's a world of difference between

Solitude and Loneliness.

Solitude restores the body and the mind.

Lonelinesss depletes them.

Solitude is something you choose.
It's being alone without feeling lonely.
Loneliness is a powerful feeling of emptiness.
A sense of isolation.
Everyone experiences both at some time.
They are often used interchangeably.
Both imply being singular.
But the resemblance ends there.

Loneliness is a negative state of mind, a sense of isolation — a feeling that something or someone is missing. It makes us feel vulnerable, introspective, self conscious. It's possible to feel lonely when surrounded by people. Alone in a crowd is a really lonely place to be. People who live alone don't have a monopoly on loneliness.

You can feel lonely in any relationship.

The emotions of loneliness feel harsh, like a punishment. It makes us feel as if we are deficient in some way. It's a feeling of discontent, a sense of estrangement, a heightened awareness of aloneness. It's stronger than the feeling of wanting company or the urge to share eating out, a weekend away, or concert.

Making the most of solitude has great rewards. Solitude means being alone without feeling lonely. Solitude has produced great literature, music, art and inventions. Inventor Issac Newton, philosophers Descartes, Kant and Nietzsche, and author Germaine Greer are just some of the world's greatest thinkers who've lived on their own. Others who spent crucial stages of their creativeness alone include the composer Beethoven, artists Da Vinci, Michelangelo, and Goya, writers Kipling, Henry James, Karen Blixen, Jane Austen and Beatrix Potter, while Coco Chanel used her solitary time to design with originality.

Solitude is a positive and constructive engagement with yourself that leads to self-awareness. It's desirable. Being alone in your own wonderful and sufficient company is time that can be spent creatively or for reflection, soul searching, and pure enjoyment. Solitary time is something worth cultivating, learning to appreciate. Time alone to encourage your imagination, concentration and discipline brings with it a peacefulness that stems from an inner richness. Seldom boredom. Enjoying the quiet and whatever it brings provides sustenance. It refreshes and provides an opportunity to renew and replenish. It gives us the chance to regain our perspective and is a necessary counterpoint to intimacy. We all need periods of solitude. Just the amount varies.

There are some people who prefer to keep to themselves altogether. To be solitary, they're often called shy. They're not introverts, they just like their own company. They've nothing against love, may be careful about it, and see themselves as complete. They don't require validation from anyone else. They're self-affirming and we can learn from them.

Instructions for life

The origin of this list is unknown. It winged its way into my life and around the internet at the beginning of the millennium. The email I received claimed it was the Dalai Lama's list, but that's not been proven. Besides, it's hard to imagine him tip tapping away at a computer keyboard and sending it to all and sundry, especially as it came with a claim that if you send it on your life will improve. So as far as I'm concerned they are written by anon and I thank anon for them. I had these words pinned up on my inspiration board for a while after I first received them.

Ten years on I still think the message is a good one to pass on. I can't guarantee your life will improve, but I know mine has since first reading them.

1. Take into account that great love and great achievements involve great risk.
2. When you lose don't lose the lesson.
3. Follow the three Rs:
   respect for self, respect for others and responsibility for your actions.
4. Remember that not getting what you want is sometimes a wonderful stroke of luck.
5. Learn the rules so you know how to break them properly.
6. Don't let a little dispute injure a great friendship.
7. Open your arms to change, but don't let go of your values.
8. Remember that silence is sometimes the best answer.
9. Live a good honourable life. Then when you get older and think back you'll be able to enjoy it a second time.
10. In disagreements with loved ones, deal only with the current situation. Don't bring up the past.
11. Share your knowledge. It's a way to achieve immortality.
12. Be gentle with the earth.
13. Once a year, go somewhere you've never been before.
14. Remember the best relationship is one in which your love for each other exceeds your need for each other.
15. Judge your success by what you had to give up in order to get it.
16. Approach love and cooking with reckless abandon.

When I read a book I want to know a little about the person behind it. So what can I tell you about me that I haven't already?

My travels have heightened my awareness. An awareness that we are all more alike than we sometimes realise, and a desire to be non-judgemental. A need to share a feeling of connectedness was the catalyst for what you now hold in your hands. I wanted to start a conversation. One about being equal and valued.

I'm not trained as an analyst of any kind. My qualification is life. My life. Thankfully I've arrived at a place that allows me to live in the moment. This hasn't happened automatically, or easily, but by rising to life's challenges. By learning to accept what is, was, and what could be. By taking risks, asking for support and reminding myself that I'm never alone, that I have someone to count on. Me.

I was born the youngest, of four, and fortunately for me, felt wanted and loved. My sister told me, when I was about seven or eight, that she felt I got it right choosing to be a girl. She said that's who my father had wanted to balance the family. Two of each. She's probably right. He was a chartered accountant. I most certainly have not inherited his love of figures and know it was the right choice to arrive as a girl because I adore being a woman. Amongst other female delights, especially the friendships, it has allowed me to be a mother.

I'm lucky. The only thing I didn't enjoy about my childhood was going to boarding school for my high school years, despite art and craft being given a healthy respect within the curriculum. I felt awkward, shy, and vulnerable.

Being the baby of the family and a shrinking violet amongst extroverts left me a lot of room for growth. Like all of us, life has delivered both good and bad. I'm sure everyone suffers what feel like injustices, things we have no power over. I like to think the reason life's thrown me hard things is so I can grow from those experiences. I am far from unique in having to learn how to accept things I didn't wish for, that I wish hadn't happened. I'm glad I've allowed myself to feel and have had the opportunity to rise to challenges. I've made mistakes and feel as though I have learned from them too. I consider them valuable lessons. I believe there will be more to come. I've also learnt that no matter what happens, or how bad things seem, there are second chances.

Early on I studied dress design and when I returned to study recently I loved being a mature-aged fine arts student. I believe in a balance in life, working for a living and giving back, and always dreamed of travelling. Inspired architecture is something I cross the world for. My greatest luxuries are a cup of tea in bed, feeling the sun on my back and sleeping in a tent. Paper, books, and textiles of any age are addictions, blue and white bowls a weakness.

I'm a home-making consultant, photographer, cook, passionate traveller, garden nurturer, creative mentor, gallery stalker and guide, and a once-in-a-blue-moon inspiration to my children. I wish I painted more often, know exercise is good for me and that I should do more. Yoga too. I love pottering, without any lists. I find the scent of gardenias and tuberoses irresistible, adore the smell of an artist's studio, the sound of a brush passing over canvas, and things made by hand. I only buy things I would have liked ten years ago and know I will still like in another ten. The click of my knitting needles feels like meditation, while the click of my camera keeps me fresh. I'm terrified of roller coasters and frightened of heights, and am glad I failed to learn how to skydive. I believe in fate, the pursuit of beauty and making life enjoyable.

Creativity is my religion. My days don't feel complete unless I do something creative and I find my mood suffers when I don't. Most of the time I'm busy with small projects, helping others. I relish being at a stage in my life where I have choices. I enjoy people and peace equally and value my family and friends above all else.

There are a few things I've done that I now feel proud of because they've been a success. At the time they were just what I was doing, and trying my hardest at, to make a living. Once upon a time I was a fashion editor for *Vogue* and *Cosmopolitan*, a stylist and art director for film and still photography. I've started a television production company, The Film Business; a small hotel called The Russell in the early 80s and then a restaurant, The Bathers' Pavilion on the beach at Balmoral, in 1988. All in Sydney. Each time I've learnt on the job, having no prior training or experience, although I understood the point of difference in giving something, be it a room or a photographic image, a unique feel and in making someone feel welcome.

I believe anything is possible.

It's a matter of imagining what you can do if you really want to. Many people dream of owning a restaurant. I didn't, but did and learned a lot. I even ended up loving it. It wasn't always easy, involved a huge learning curve, the belief of others, and an audience who wanted what I had to offer. For a restaurant to have a soul it needs to have an individual feel, staff who care, and know you do too. So it is for any business. Doing something you love usually means you do it well. The love shows.

Making a home, nurturing, and having the capacity and opportunity to love are things I value. I married Andrew at twenty-two. We were married for twenty-eight years and had three wonderful children together. He was an entrepreneur who believed in me. Despite being divorced, I felt like a widow when he died and I became a single parent.

It seems to me the only thing that matters is the life you live between birth and death. Some people are given more to deal with than others, which, if you believe the Buddhist philosophy, is so we learn the lessons we didn't last time round. Whichever way you like to see it, if you're at all like me, feeling devastated is a place I won't willingly visit again. That's not to say some sadness is not a good thing. I believe when you feel sad you see things clearly as your emotions are heightened. Unhappy times have motivated me and reinforced my belief that life is totally up to me to make what I want of it.

I've found that after the steamroller has passed over me and I reinflate again, needing to deal with decisions that have to be made, and the changes, that I have a choice after all. About how I will let things affect me. A mindset if you like, and so I set to work on cultivating a positive approach, thoughts that are kind to myself, that counteract the negative ones. Change takes time and is not always easy. I have learnt that sometimes it's necessary, and important, to ask for something you feel will contribute to your happiness and create harmony.

If I think about the life I'm now living, I feel content and privileged to have it.

Thank you for choosing to read this book.

This book insisted on itself. Partly in memory of my spirited nephew, Joe, who lived a lifetime in fifteen years. He never held back.

It felt like a story that wanted to be told and was started on 28th December 2008. I heard its heartbeat and we became friends. It has gone on to make friends with others.

First there is Barbara.
She came to lunch with an idea for a different story and went away committed to this one. We have used many words to describe her role during the process. Book muse, sounding board, coach, but I like her words best. 'It's as if there is a key in Victoria's back and I occasionally wind it.' It was an entirely different kind of creative process for her. She gave it everything. There was no need to ask for more.

I am grateful for the immediate belief in *One* from Diana Hill and Kay Scarlett at Murdoch. Thank you for a winter spent discovering more about human nature and tackling writing. My words have been thoughtfully massaged by Katrina O'Brien, and I was also lucky to have Vivien Valk artfully turn my torn pages into this finished book. I'd go on any journey with them anytime. They too had help from Holly who wrangled image files.

One has taught me a lot.
About the written word. Also about myself. Like everyone, I'm not the same person I was when I was a teenager, memories have flooded back, of people and places. Also of books, of times when I have read something that opened up possibilities. It has served as a reminder that anything is possible. It celebrates and honours the understanding of self, and making the most of it.

Again friends and family helped. In ways they were aware of and many they weren't. It would not be complete without seeing their names in print but I am not going to do that. More importantly they know exactly who they are and that they have my love and heartfelt thanks.

But this book began before all this. It began when I began again seven years ago. What is it they say about seven year cycles? If I am to believe in them mine has been a stage of transformation. What once seemed so important is no longer. It's true the viewpoints I now have compared to my younger years are different. I know as you sow, you shall reap to be true and that each life situation has been brought about by my own choices.

The best choice I have made is to be a mother. This book is a celebration of my mother and is dedicated to the special three individuals who made me one. With all my love. Always. X

One last thing

The Author would like to thank and acknowledge the following people who have helped make this book possible by sharing their images or granting permission to reproduce words, some their own, others of those they represent. And a big thanks too to all the booksellers and librarians who pass by this book.

Images

12 Glenn Thomas
17 misschu
26 Georgio Morandi, *Still Life*, undated (1950), Oil on canvas, 42.5 x 47 cm, Bologna, Museo Morandi. Copyright © Giorgio Morandi/SIAE. Licensed by Viscopy, 2010.
37 Edward Hopper (American, 1882–1967), *Automat*, 1927, oil on canvas, 36 x 28⅛ in (91.4 x 71.4 cm), Des Moines Art Center Permanent Collectiuons; Purchased with funds from the Edmundson Art Foundation, Inc., 1958.2
43 Glenn Thomas
55 Luis Barragán, Gilardi House, Mexico City, 1975-77, photo: Armando Salas Portugal, © Barragan Foundation, Switzerland/ProLitteris, Zürich, Switzerland. Licensed by Viscopy, 2010.
68 Photographs by Natasha Milne, © Murdoch Books Pty Limited
68 Artwork by Annie Herron
73 Photographs by Natasha Milne, © Murdoch Books Pty Limited
73 Artwork by Victoria Alexander
74 Nathalie Lete
76 Alex Popov Architects
90 Adrian Lockhart (drawing), The Regional Assembly of Text (typewriter keys)
95 Artwork by Annie Herron
109 William Joseph
115 Professor Geoffrey Driscoll
125 William Joseph
156 Glenn Thomas
162 SugarLove Weddings
191 Adrian Lockhart
197 Photographs by Natasha Milne, © Murdoch Books Pty Limited
197 Artwork by Victoria Alexander
202 © Andy Goldsworthy. Courtesy Tim Adams & Galerie Lelong, New York
204 Photographs by Natasha Milne, © Murdoch Books Pty Limited
216 Phoebe McEvoy
229 Photographs by Natasha Milne, © Murdoch Books Pty Limited
244 Casper David Friedrich, *The Wanderer Above a Sea of Fog*, (around 1818), oil on canvas, 98 x 74 cm, Kunsthalle.
160 Melinda Conrad
212 SugarLove Weddings
248 Peter Purcell
250 Sarah Stegley
Cover Back cover: Photographs by Victoria Alexander except for African man in pink robe © Robert Caputo, Aurora Photos. Back flap: Photographs by Natasha Milne, © Murdoch Books Pty Limited.

Wonderful words

40 Excerpt from 'Bird on a Wire' from *Stranger Music: Selected Poems and Songs* by Leonard Cohen © 1993. Reprinted with permission. All rights reserved.
102 *Beyond Dogma: Dialogues & Discourses* by the Dalai Lama, edited by Marianne Dresser, English translation by Alison Anderson, published by North Atlantic Books, copyright © 1996 by North Atlantic Books. Reprinted by permission of the publisher.
103 Jack Kornfield, 1993, *A Path with Heart: A Guide Through the Perils and Promises of Spiritual Life*, Bantam Books (an imprint of Random House) Random House, Inc.
140 Craig Silvey, *Jasper Jones*, Allen & Unwin, Australia, 2009.
159 Picasso quote © Succession Picasso 2010
163 Excerpt from 'Hallelujah' from *Stranger Music: Selected Poems and Songs* by Leonard Cohen © 1993. Reprinted with permission. All rights reserved.
185 Dorothy S. Hunt, *Only This!*
202 Quote from 'Natural Talent', Tim Adams, *The Observer*, Sunday 11 March 2007 © Andy Goldsworthy. Courtesy Tim Adams & Galerie Lelong, New York
224 Bertrand Russell, *The Conquest of Happiness,* Part 11: Causes of happiness, Chapter 10: Is happiness still possible, Taylor and Francis, © The Bertrand Russell Peace Foundation Ltd.
234 Brief (stand-alone) quote from p.311 from *The Freedom Manifesto* by Tom Hodgkinson. Copyright © 2006 by Tom Hodginson. Reprinted by permission of HarperCollins Publishers. Also from *Beyond Dogma: Dialogues & Discourses* by the Dalai Lama, edited by Marianne Dresser, English translation by Alison Anderson, published by North Atlantic Books © 1996 by North Atlantic Books. Reprinted by permission of the publisher.

First published in 2010. This edition published in 2019 by
Murdoch Books, an imprint of Allen and Unwin

Murdoch Books Australia
83 Alexander Street, Crows Nest NSW 2065
Phone: +61 (0)2 8425 0100
murdochbooks.com.au
info@murdochbooks.com.au

Murdoch Books UK
Ormond House, 26–27 Boswell Street, London WC1N 3JZ
Phone: +44 (0) 20 8785 5995
murdochbooks.co.uk
info@murdochbooks.co.uk

For corporate orders & custom publishing, contact our business development team at salesenquiries@murdochbooks.com.au

Publisher: Diana Hill
Designer: Vivien Valk
Project Editor: Katrina O'Brien
Production: Alexandra Gonzalez

A cataloguing-in-publication entry is available from the catalogue of the National Library of Australia at nla.gov.au
A catalogue record for this book is available from the British Library

ISBN 9 781 76052 545 3 Australia
ISBN 9 781 91163 266 5 UK

Printed by Imago in Singapore.